JESUS SAID

A DAILY DEVOTIONAL INSPIRED
BY THE WORDS OF CHRIST

Compiled By
LOUISE THORNTON HORNSBY

THE WORD OF GOD, Inc.
2016 Sandtown Rd.
Atlanta, GA 30311
Contact: 404-758-0356

Copyright © 2018 by THE WORD OF GOD Inc, and Louise T. Hornsby All Rights Reserved

No part of this publication may be reproduced, stored in a retrieval system, or transmitted in any form by any means electronic, mechanical, photocopying, recording, scanning or otherwise except as permitted under Section 107 or 108 of the 1976 United States Copyright Act, without the prior written permission of the Publisher.

For information address | Louise T. Hornsby at louisethornsby@yahoo.com

For information about JESUS SAID | Contact Author

Created in the United States of America

Disclaimer
Limit of Liability/Disclaimer of Warranty: While the publisher and author have used their best efforts in preparing this book, they make no representations or warranties with respect to the accuracy or completeness of the contents of this book and specifically disclaim any implied warranties or merchantability or fitness for a particular purpose. No warranties may be created or extended by the author's representatives or written sales materials. Author acknowledges that Dr. Fred Jones and Publish Me Now University is not the publisher of this title or content. Author represent and warrant that author is the publisher of this title including all content therein and in any case, author will bear the full and ultimate responsibility for the publication and general distribution of this book.

*For the Word of God is quick, and
powerful, and sharper than any two-edged
sword, piercing even to the dividing
asunder of soul and spirit, and of the joints
and marrow, and is a discerner of
the thoughts and intents of the heart*
~ Hebrews 4:12

Dedication

This book is dedicated to everyone who wants to know the words of Christ Jesus and how to live according to his words.

Special Thanks

Special thanks to God, my Father; Jesus,
my Savior and lover of my soul;
and the Holy Spirit, my Guide.

I also want to thank Jacqueline Price,
Jenese Hornsby, Breanna Wilson, and
Lawrence Tyler Hornsby, my helpers and
editors. I appreciate your dedication in
helping me complete this work. I feel honored
to work with such a great team.
Dr. Fred Jones, thanks to you and your team
for coaching me through this writing
and publishing process!

INTRODUCTION

Because of the many interpretations and opinions of what Jesus said, it is very important to know the words of Jesus for yourself. I felt the need to know "What Jesus Said" for myself and thought how wonderful it would be to read a daily journal with the words Jesus spoke throughout the Bible. I have compiled as a daily journal the words spoken by Jesus, so that we will all learn to follow Jesus in spirit and in truth. I pray that each day you read this book you will be inspired, blessed and become more like Jesus. These Words said and spoken by Jesus are more effective when spoken or read aloud.

Louise Thornton Hornsby

January 1
JESUS SAID:

1. *Suffer it to be now, for thus it becometh us to fulfill all righteousness.* - **Matthew 3:15**

2. *It is written, man shall not live by bread alone.* - **Matthew 4:4**

3. *But by every word that proceeded out of the mouth of God.* - **Matthew 4:4**

4. *It is written again, thou shalt not tempt the Lord thy God.* - **Matthew 4:7**

5. *Get thee hence Satan, for it is written, thou shalt worship the Lord thy God.* - **Matthew 4:10**

6. *And him only shalt thou serve.* - **Matthew 4:10**

7. *Repent, for the kingdom of Heaven is at hand.* - **Matthew 4:17**

8. *Follow me, and I will make you fishers of men.* - **Matthew 4:19**

9. *Blessed are the poor in spirit.* - **Matthew 5:3**

10. *For theirs is the kingdom of Heaven.* - **Matthew 5:3**

January 2

JESUS SAID:

1. Ye are the salt of the earth. - **Matthew 5:13**

2. But if the salt has lost his savour, wherewith shall it be salted. - **Matthew 5:13**

3. It is thenceforth good for nothing but to be cast out. - **Matthew 5:13**

4. And to be trodden under foot of men. - **Matthew 5:13**

5. Ye are the light of the world. - **Matthew 5:14**

6. A city that is set on a hill cannot be hid. - **Matthew 5:14**

7. Neither do men light a candle and put it under a bushel, but on a candlestick. - **Matthew 5:15**

8. And it giveth light unto all that are in the house. - **Matthew 5:15**

9. Let your light so shine before men, that they may see your good works. - **Matthew 5:16**

10. And glorify your Father which is in Heaven. - **Matthew 5:16**

January 3

JESUS SAID:

1. *Think not that I come to destroy the law or the prophets.*
   - **Matthew 5:17**
2. *I am not come to destroy but to fulfill.* - **Matthew 5:17**
3. *For verily I say unto you, till Heaven and earth pass.*
   - **Matthew 5:18**
4. *One jot or one tittle shall in no wise pass from the law, till all be fulfilled.* - **Matthew 5:18**
5. *Whosoever therefore break one of these least commandments, and shall teach men so, he shall be called the least in the kingdom of Heaven.* - **Matthew 5:19**
6. *But whosoever shall do and teach them, the same shall be called great in the kingdom of Heaven.* - **Matthew 5:19**
7. *For I say unto you, that except your righteousness shall exceed the righteousness of the scribes and Pharisees, ye shall in no case enter into the kingdom of Heaven.*
   - **Matthew 5:20**
8. *Ye have heard it was said by them of old time.*
   - **Matthew 5:21**
9. *Thou shalt not kill, and whosoever shall kill shall be in danger of the judgement.* - **Matthew 5:21**
10. *But I say unto you, that whosoever is angry with his brother without a cause shall be in danger of judgement.*
    - **Matthew 5:22**

January 4

JESUS SAID:

1. And whosoever shall say to his brother Raca, shall be in danger of the council. - **Matthew 5:22**

2. But whosoever shall say, thou fool, shall be in danger of hell fire. - **Matthew 5:22**

3. Therefore if thou bring thy gifts to the altar, and there remember that thy brother hath ought against thee. - **Matthew 5:23**

4. Leave there thy gift before the altar, and go thy way. - **Matthew 5:24**

5. First be reconciled to thy brother. - **Matthew 5:24**

6. And then come and offer thy gift. - **Matthew 5:24**

7. Agree with thine adversary quickly, while thou art in the way with him. - **Matthew 5:25**

8. Lest at any time the adversary deliver thee to the judge. - **Matthew 5:25**

9. And the judge deliver thee to the officer. - **Matthew 5:25**

10. And thou be cast into prison. - **Matthew 5:25**

January 5

JESUS SAID:

1. Verily I say unto thee, thou shalt by no means come out thence. - **Matthew 5:26**

2. Till thou hast paid the uttermost farthing. - **Matthew 5:26**

3. Ye have heard that it was said by them of old time. - **Matthew 5:27**

4. Thou shalt not commit adultery. - **Matthew 5:27**

5. But I say unto you. - **Matthew 5:28**

6. That whosoever looketh on a woman to lust after her hath committed adultery with her already in his heart. - **Matthew 5:28**

7. And if thy right eye offend thee, pluck it out, cast it from thee. - **Matthew 5:29**

8. For it is profitable for thee that one of thy members should perish. - **Matthew 5:29**

9. And not that thy whole body should be cast into hell. –**Matthew 5:29**

10. And if thy right hand offend thee, cut it off, and cast it from thee; for it is more profitable for thee that one of thy members should perish, and not thy whole body should be cast into hell. - **Matthew 5:30**

January 6

JESUS SAID:

1. It hath been said whosoever shall put away his wife, let him give her a writing of divorcement. - **Matthew 5:31**

2. But I say unto you, that whosoever shall put away his wife, saving for the cause of fornication, causes her to commit adultery. - **Matthew 5:32**

3. And whosoever shall marry her that is divorced committeth adultery. - **Matthew 5:32**

4. Again, ye have heard that it hath been said by them of old time. - **Matthew 5:33**

5. Thou shalt not forswear thyself, but shalt perform unto the Lord thine oaths. - **Matthew 5:33**

6. But I say unto you swear not at all. - **Matthew 5:34**

7. Neither by Heaven, for it is God's throne. - **Matthew 5:34**

8. Nor by the earth, for it is his footstool. - **Matthew 5:35**

9. Neither by Jerusalem for it is the city of the great king. - **Matthew 5:35**

10. Neither shalt thou swear by thy head, because thou canst not make one hair white or black. - **Matthew 5:36**

January 7

JESUS SAID:

1. But let your communication be, yea, yea; nay, nay.
   - **Matthew 5:37**

2. For whatsoever is more than these cometh of evil.
   - **Matthew 5:37**

3. Take heed that ye do not your alms before men. - **Matthew 6:1**

4. To be seen of them. - **Matthew 6:1**

5. Otherwise ye have no reward of your Father which is in Heaven. - **Matthew 6:1**

6. Therefore, when thou doest thine alms, do not sound a trumpet before thee. - **Matthew 6:2**

7. As the hypocrites do in the synagogues and in the streets that they may have glory of men. - **Matthew 6:2**

8. Verily I say unto you, they have their rewards. - **Matthew 6:2**

9. When thou doest thine alms, let not thy left hand know what thy right hand doeth. - **Matthew 6:3**

10. That thine alms may be in secret, and thy Father which seeth in secret himself shall reward thee openly. - **Matthew 6:4**

January 8

JESUS SAID:

1. For if ye forgive men their trespasses, your Heavenly Father will also forgive you. - **Matthew 6:14**

2. But if ye forgive not men their trespasses, neither will your Father forgive your trespasses. - **Matthew 6:15**

3. Moreover when ye fast, be not as the hypocrites of a sad countenance. - **Matthew 6:16**

4. For they disfigure their faces, that they may appear unto men to fast. - **Matthew 6:16**

5. Verily I say unto you, they have their reward. - **Matthew 6:16**

6. But thou, when thou fastest, anoint thine head, and wash thy face. - **Matthew 6:17**

7. That thou appear not unto men to fast, but unto thy Father. - **Matthew 6:18**

8. And thy Father which seeth in secret, shall reward thee openly. - **Matthew 6:18**

9. Which of you by taking thought can add one cubit unto his statute. - **Matthew 6:27**

10. Judge not that ye be not judged. - **Matthew 7:1**

January 9

JESUS SAID:

1. For with what judgement ye judge, ye shall be judged. - **Matthew 7:2**

2. And with what measure ye mete, it shall be measured to you again. - **Matthew 7:2**

3. And why beholdest thou the mote that is in thy brother's eye. - **Matthew 7:2**

4. But considerest not the beam that is in thine own eye? - **Matthew 7:2**

5. Or how wilt thou say to thy brother, let me pull out the mote out of thine eye. - **Matthew 7:4**

6. And behold, a beam is in thine own eye? - **Matthew 7:4**

7. Thou hypocrite, first cast out the beam out of thine own eye. - **Matthew 7:5**

8. And then shalt thou see clearly to cast out the mote out of thy brother's eye. - **Matthew 7:5**

9. Give not that which is holy unto the dogs, neither cast ye your pearls before swine. - **Matthew 7:6**

10. Lest they trample them under their feet, and turn again and rend you. - **Matthew 7:6**

January 10

JESUS SAID:

1. Ask, and it shall be given you, seek, and ye shall find. - **Matthew 7:7**

2. Knock, and it shall be opened unto you. - **Matthew 7:7**

3. For everyone that asketh receiveth. - **Matthew 7:8**

4. And he that seeketh findeth. - **Matthew 7:8**

5. And to him that knocketh it shall be opened. - **Matthew 7:8**

6. Or what man is there of you, whom if his son ask bread will give him a stone? - **Matthew 7:9**

7. Or if he ask a fish, will he give him a serpent? - **Matthew 7:10**

8. If ye then, being evil, know how to give good gifts unto your children. - **Matthew 7:11**

9. How much more shall your Father which is in Heaven give good things to them that ask him? - **Matthew 7:11**

10. Therefore all things whatsoever ye would that men should do to you, do ye even to them; for this is the law and the prophets. - **Matthew 7:12**

January 11

JESUS SAID:

1. Even so every good tree bringeth forth good fruit.
   - **Matthew 7:17**

2. But a corrupt tree bringeth forth evil fruit. - **Matthew 7:17**

3. A good tree cannot bring forth evil fruit. - **Matthew 7:18**

4. Neither can a corrupt tree bring forth good fruit.
   - **Matthew 7:18**

5. Every tree that bringeth not forth good fruit is hewn down and cast into the fire. - **Matthew 7:19**

6. Wherefore by their fruits ye shall know them. - **Matthew 7:20**

7. Not everyone that saith unto me Lord, Lord shall enter into the kingdom of Heaven. - **Matthew 7:21**

8. But he that doeth the will of my Father which is in Heaven. - **Matthew 7:21**

9. Many will say to me in that day, Lord, Lord, have we not prophesied in thy name and in thy name have cast out devils? And in thy name done many wonderful works. - **Matthew 7:22**

10. And then will I profess unto them, I never knew you, depart from me ye that work iniquity. - **Matthew 7:23**

January 12

JESUS SAID:

1. Therefore whosoever heareth these sayings of mine and doeth them, I will liken him unto a wise man. - **Matthew 7:24**

2. Which build his house upon a rock. - **Matthew 7:24**

3. And the rain descended and the flood came, and the wind blew, and beat upon that house and it fell not. - **Matthew 7:25**

4. For it was founded upon a rock. - **Matthew 7:25**

5. And everyone that heareth these sayings of mine, and doeth them not, shall be likened unto a foolish man. - **Matthew 7:26**

6. Which build his house upon the sand. - **Matthew 7:26**

7. And the rain descended, and the floods came, and the wind blew, and beat upon that house. - **Matthew 7:27**

8. And it fell, and great was the fall of it. - **Matthew 7:27**

9. I will be thou clean. - **Matthew 8:3**

10. See, thou tell no man; but go thy way, shew thyself to the priest, and offer the gift that Moses commanded, for a testimony unto them. - **Matthew 8:4**

January 13

JESUS SAID:

1. I will come and heal him. - **Matthew 8:7**

2. Verily I say unto you, I have not found so great faith, no not in Israel. - **Matthew 8:10**

3. Behold, I send you forth as a sheep in the midst of wolves. - **Matthew 10:16**

4. Be therefore wise as serpents, and harmless as doves. - **Matthew 10:16**

5. But beware of men, for they will deliver you up to the councils. - **Matthew 10:17**

6. And they will scourge you in their synagogues. - **Matthew 10:17**

7. And ye shall be brought before governors and kings for my sake. - **Matthew 10:18**

8. For a testimony against them and the Gentiles. - **Matthew 10:18**

9. But when they deliver you up, take no thought how or what ye shall speak. - **Matthew 10:19**

10. For it shall be given you in that same hour what ye shall speak. - **Matthew 10:19**

January 14

JESUS SAID:

1. For it is not ye that speak, but the Spirit of your Father which speaketh in you. - **Matthew 10:20**

2. And the brother shall deliver up the brother to death. - **Matthew 10:21**

3. And the father the child. - **Matthew 10:21**

4. And the children shall rise up against their parents, and cause them to be put to death. - **Matthew 10:21**

5. And ye shall be hated of all men for my name's sake. - **Matthew 10:22**

6. But he that endureth to the end and shall be saved. - **Matthew 10:22**

7. But when they persecute you in the city, flee ye to another. - **Matthew 10:23**

8. For verily I say unto you. - **Matthew 10:23**

9. Ye shall not have gone over the cities of Israel. - **Matthew 10:23**

10. Till the Son of man be come. - **Matthew 10:23**

January 15

JESUS SAID:

1. The disciple is not above his master. - **Matthew 10:24**

2. Nor the servant above his lord. - **Matthew 10:24**

3. It is enough for the disciple that he be as his master, and the servant as his lord. - **Matthew 10:25**

4. If they have called the master of the house Beelzebub, how much more shall they call them of his household.
   - **Matthew 10:25**

5. Fear them not therefore. - **Matthew 10:26**

6. For there is nothing covered, that shall not be revealed.
   - **Matthew 10:26**

7. And hid, that shall not be known. - **Matthew 10:26**

8. What I tell you in darkness, that speak ye in light.
   - **Matthew 10:27**

9. And what ye hear in the ear, that preach ye upon the housetops. - **Matthew 10:27**

10. And fear not them which kill the body, but rather fear him which is able to destroy both soul and body in hell.
    - **Matthew 10:28**

January 16

JESUS SAID:

1. Are not two sparrows sold for a farthing? - **Matthew 10:29**

2. And one of them shall not fall on the ground without your Father. - **Matthew 10:29**

3. But the very hairs on your head are all numbered. - **Matthew 10:30**

4. Fear ye not therefore. - **Matthew 10:31**

5. Ye are of more value than many sparrows. - **Matthew 10:31**

6. Whosoever therefore shall confess me before men. - **Matthew 10:32**

7. Him will I confess also before my Father which is in Heaven. - **Matthew 10:32**

8. But whosoever shall deny me before men. - **Matthew 10:33**

9. Him will I also deny before my Father which is in Heaven. - **Matthew 10:33**

10. Think not that I am come to send peace on earth, I came not to send peace, but a sword. - **Matthew 10:34**

January 17

JESUS SAID:

1. Think not that I am come to send peace on the earth. - **Matthew 10:34**

2. I came not to send peace, but a sword. - **Matthew 10:34**

3. For I am come to set a man at variance against his father. - **Matthew 10:35**

4. And the daughter against her mother. - **Matthew 10:35**

5. And the daughter in law against her mother in law. - **Matthew 10:35**

6. And a man's foes shall be they of his own household. - **Matthew 10:36**

7. He that loveth father or mother more than me is not worthy of me. - **Matthew 10:37**

8. And he that loveth son or daughter more than me is not worthy of me. - **Matthew 10:37**

9. And he that taketh not his cross, and followeth after me is not worthy of me. - **Matthew 10:38**

10. He that findeth his life shall lose it and he that loseth his life for my sake shall find it. - **Matthew 10:39**

January 18

JESUS SAID:

1. He that receiveth you, receiveth me. - **Matthew 10:40**

2. And he that receiveth me receiveth him that sent me. - **Matthew 10:40**

3. He that receiveth a prophet in the name of a prophet shall receive a prophet's reward. - **Matthew 10:41**

4. And he that receiveth a righteous man in the name of a righteous man shall receive a righteous man's reward. - **Matthew 10:41**

5. And whosoever shall give to drink unto one of these little ones a cup of cold water only in the name of a disciple, verily I say unto you, he shall in no wise lose his reward. - **Matthew 10:42**

6. Go, and shew John again these things which ye do, hear and see. - **Matthew 11:4**

7. The blind receive their sight. - **Matthew 11:5**

8. The lepers are cleansed. - **Matthew 11:5**

9. The deaf hear. - **Matthew 11:5**

10. The dead are raised up. - **Matthew 11:5**

January 19

JESUS SAID:

1. And the poor have the gospel preached to them.
   - **Matthew 11:5**

2. And blessed is he, whosoever shall not be offended in me.
   - **Matthew 11:6**

3. What went ye out into the wilderness to see. - **Matthew 11:7**

4. A reed shaken with the wind? - **Matthew 11:7**

5. But what went ye out to see? - **Matthew 11:8**

6. A man clothed in soft raiment? - **Matthew 11:8**

7. Behold, they that wear soft clothing are in kings' houses.
   - **Matthew 11:8**

8. But what went ye out for to see? - **Matthew 11:9**

9. A prophet? Yea, I say unto you, and more than a prophet.
   - **Matthew 11:9**

10. For this is he, of whom it is written, behold, I send my messenger before thy face, which shall prepare thy way before thee. - **Matthew 11:10**

January 20

JESUS SAID:

1. Verily I say unto you, among them that are born of women there hath not risen a greater than John the Baptist.
   - **Matthew 11:11**

2. Notwithstanding he that is least in the kingdom of Heaven is greater than he. - **Matthew 11:11**

3. And from the days of John the Baptist until now the kingdom of Heaven suffereth violence, and the violent take it by force.
   - **Matthew 11:12**

4. For all the prophets and the law prophesied until John.
   - **Matthew 11:13**

5. And if you will receive it, this is Elias, which was for to come.
   - **Matthew 11:14**

6. And he that has ears to hear, let him hear. - **Matthew 11:15**

7. But whereunto shall I liken this generation? - **Matthew 11:16**

8. It is like unto children sitting in the markets, and calling unto their fellows. - **Matthew 11:16**

9. And saying we have piped unto you, and ye have not danced.
   - **Matthew 11:17**

10. We have mourned unto you, and ye have not lamented. - **Matthew 11:17**

January 21

JESUS SAID:

1. For John came neither eating nor drinking, and they say, he hath a devil. - **Matthew 11:18**

2. The Son of man came eating and drinking and they say, behold a man gluttonous and a winebibber, a friend of publicans and sinners. - **Matthew 11:19**

3. But wisdom is justified of her children. - **Matthew 11:19**

4. Woe unto thee, Chorazin! woe unto thee, Bethsaida. - **Matthew 11:21**

5. For if the mighty works which were done in you, had been done in Tyre and Sidon. - **Matthew 11:21**

6. They would have repented long ago in sackcloth and ashes. - **Matthew 11:21**

7. But I say unto you. - **Matthew 11:22**

8. It shall be more tolerable for Tyre and Sidon at the day of judgement than for you. - **Matthew 11:22**

9. And thou Capernaum, which art exalted unto Heaven, shalt be brought down to hell. - **Matthew 11:23**

10. For if the mighty works, which have been done in thee had been done in Sodom it would have remained until this day. - **Matthew 11:23**

January 22

JESUS SAID:

1. But I say unto you. - **Matthew 11:24**

2. That it shall be more tolerable for the land of Sodom in the Day of Judgment than for thee. - **Matthew 11:25**

3. I thank thee, O Father, Lord of Heaven and earth. - **Matthew 11:25**

4. Because thou hast hid these things from the wise and prudent and hast revealed them unto babes. - **Matthew 11:25**

5. Even so, Father; for so it seemed good in thy sight. - **Matthew 11:26**

6. All things are delivered unto me of my Father, and no man knoweth the Son but the Father. - **Matthew 11:27**

7. Neither knoweth any man the Father, save the Son. - **Matthew 11:27**

8. And he to whomsoever the Son will reveal. - **Matthew 11:27**

9. Come unto me, all ye that labor and are heavy laden, and I will give you rest. - **Matthew 11:28**

10. Take my yoke upon you, and learn of me; for I am meek and lowly in heart; and ye shall find rest unto your souls, for my yoke is easy and my burden light. - **Matthew 11:29-30**

January 23

JESUS SAID:

1. Have ye not read what David did? - **Matthew 12:3**

2. When he was an hungred. - **Matthew 12:3**

3. And they that were with him. - **Matthew 12:3**

4. How he entered into the house of God. - **Matthew 12:4**

5. And did eat the shewbread which was not lawful for him to eat. - **Matthew 12:4**

6. Neither for them which were with him. - **Matthew 12:4**

7. But only for the priest. - **Matthew 12:4**

8. Or have you not read in the law. - **Matthew 12:5**

9. How that on the Sabbath days the priest in the temple profaned the Sabbath, and are blameless? - **Matthew 12:5**

10. But I say unto you that in this place is one greater. - **Matthew 12:6**

January 24

JESUS SAID:

1. But if ye had known what this meaneth, I will have mercy, and not sacrifice. - **Matthew 12:7**

2. Ye would not have condemned the guiltless. - **Matthew 12:7**

3. For the Son of man is Lord even of the Sabbath day. - **Matthew 12:8**

4. What man shall be among you, that have one sheep, and if it fall into a pit on the Sabbath day, will he not lay hold on it and lift it out? - **Matthew 12:11**

5. How much then is a man better than a sheep. - **Matthew 12:12**

6. Wherefore it is lawful to do well on the Sabbath day. - **Matthew 12:12**

7. Stretch forth thine hand. - **Matthew 12:13**

8. Have ye understood all these things? - **Matthew 13:51**

9. Therefore every scribe which is instructed into the kingdom of Heaven is like a man that is a householder. - **Matthew 13:52**

10. Which bringeth forth out of his treasure things new and old. - **Matthew 13:52**

January 25

JESUS SAID:

1. Get thee behind me, Satan. - **Matthew 16:23**

2. Thou art an offense to me. - **Matthew 16:23**

3. For thou savourest not the things that be of God. - **Matthew 16:23**

4. But those that be of men. - **Matthew 16:23**

5. Tell the vision to no man, until the Son of man be risen from the dead. - **Matthew 17:9**

6. Elias truly shall come, and restore all things. - **Matthew 17:11**

7. But I say unto you, that Elias is come already, and they knew him not, but have done unto him whatsoever they listed. - **Matthew 17:12**

8. Likewise shall also the Son of man suffer of them. - **Matthew 17:12**

9. O Faithless and perverse generation, how long shall I be with you? - **Matthew 17:17**

10. How long shall I suffer you? Bring him hither to me. - **Matthew 17:17**

January 26

JESUS SAID:

1. Because of your unbelief, for verily I say unto you. - **Matthew 17:20**

2. If ye have faith as a grain of mustard seed. - **Matthew 17:20**

3. Ye shall say to this mountain, remove hence to yonder place and it shall remove. - **Matthew 17:20**

4. And nothing shall be impossible to you. - **Matthew 17:20**

5. Howbeit this kind goeth not out but by prayer and fasting. - **Matthew 17:21**

6. The Son of man shall be betrayed into the hands of men. - **Matthew 17:22**

7. And they shall kill him and the third day he shall be raised again. - **Matthew 17:25**

8. What thinkest thou, Simon? - **Matthew 17:25**

9. Of whom do all the kings of the earth take custom or tribute? - **Matthew 17:25**

10. Of their own children, or of strangers? Then the children are free. - **Matthew 17:25-26**

January 27

JESUS SAID:

1. Not withstanding, lest we should offend them go thou to the sea, and cast an hook, and take up the fish that first cometh up. - **Matthew 17:27**
2. And when thou hast opened his mouth, thou shalt find a piece of money. - **Matthew 17:27**
3. That take and give unto them for me and thee. - **Matthew 17:29**
4. Verily I say unto you, except ye be converted. - **Matthew 18:3**
5. And become as little children, ye shall not enter into the kingdom of Heaven. - **Matthew 18:3**
6. And whosoever therefore shall humble himself as this little child, the same is greatest in the kingdom of Heaven. - **Matthew 18:4**
7. And whoso shall receive one such little child in my name, receiveth me. - **Matthew 18:5**
8. But whoso shall offend one of these little ones which believe in me. - **Matthew 18:6**
9. It were better for him that a millstone were hanged about his neck, and that he were drowned in the depth of the sea. - **Matthew 18:6**
10. Woe unto the world because of offences for it must needs be that offences come; but woe to that man by whom the offence cometh. - **Matthew 18:7**

January 28

JESUS SAID:

1. Wherefore if thy hand or thy foot offend thee, cut them off, and cast them from thee. - **Matthew 18:8**
2. It is better for thee to enter into life halt or maimed, rather than having two hands or two feet to be cast into everlasting fire. - **Matthew 18:8**
3. And if thine eye offend thee, pluck it out and cast it from thee. - **Matthew 18:9**
4. It is better for thee to enter into life with one eye, rather than having two eyes to be cast into hell fire. - **Matthew 18:9**
5. Take heed that ye despise not one of these little ones. - **Matthew 18:10**
6. For I say unto you, that in Heaven their angels do always behold the face of my Father which is in Heaven. - **Matthew 18:10**
7. For the Son of man is come to save that which is lost. - **Matthew 18:11**
8. How think ye? If a man have a hundred sheep and one of them be gone astray. - **Matthew 18:12**
9. Doth he, not leave the ninety and nine and goeth into the mountains, and seeketh that which is gone astray? - **Matthew 18:12**
10. And if so be that he find it, verily I say unto you he rejoiceth more of that sheep than of the ninety and nine which went not astray. - **Matthew 18:13**

January 29

JESUS SAID:

1. Even so it is not the will of your Father which is in Heaven that one of these little ones should perish. - **Matthew 18:14**

2. Moreover if thy brother shall trespass against thee. - **Matthew 18:15**

3. Go and tell him his fault between thee and him alone. - **Matthew 18:15**

4. If he shall hear thee thou hast gained thy brother. - **Matthew 18:15**

5. But if he will not hear thee, then take with thee one or two more. - **Matthew 18:16**

6. That in the mouth of two or three witnesses every word may be established. - **Matthew 18:16**

7. And if he shall neglect to hear them, tell it to church. - **Matthew 18:17**

8. But if he neglect to hear the church, let his be unto thee as a heathen man and a publican. - **Matthew 18:17**

9. Verily I say unto you, whatsoever ye shall bind on earth shall be bound in Heaven. - **Matthew 18:18**

10. And whatsoever ye shall loose on earth shall be loosed in Heaven. - **Matthew 18:18**

January 30

JESUS SAID:

1. Again I say unto you, that if two of you shall agree on earth as touching anything that they shall ask. - **Matthew 18:19**

2. It shall be done for them of my Father which is in Heaven. - **Matthew 18:19**

3. For where two or three are gathered in my name. - **Matthew 18:20**

4. There am I in the midst of them. - **Matthew 18:20**

5. I say not unto thee, until seven times, but until seventy times seven. - **Matthew 18:22**

6. Therefore is the kingdom of Heaven likened unto a certain king, which would take account of his servants? - **Matthew 18:23**

7. And when he had begun to reckon, one was brought unto him which owed him ten thousand talents. - **Matthew 18:24**

8. But forasmuch as he had not to pay. - **Matthew 18:25**

9. His Lord commanded him to be sold, and his wife and children, and all that he had, and payment to be made. - **Matthew 18:25**

10. The servant therefore fell down, and worshipped him saying, Lord have patience with me, and I will pay thee all. - **Matthew 18:26**

January 31

JESUS SAID:

1. Then the lord of that servant was moved with compassion, and loosed him and forgave him the debt. - **Matthew 18:27**
2. But that same servant went out and found one of his fellow servants, which owed him an hundred pence. - **Matthew 18:28**
3. And he laid his hands on him, and took him by throat, saying, pay me that thou owest. - **Matthew 18:28**
4. And his fellow servant fell down at his feet, and besought him saying, have patience with me, and I will pay thee all. - **Matthew 18:29**
5. And he would not but went and cast him into prison, till he should pay the debt. - **Matthew 18:30**
6. So when his fellow servants saw what was done, they were very sorry, and came and told unto their lord all that was done. - **Matthew 18:31**
7. Then his lord, after that he had called him, said unto him, o thou wicked servant, I forgave thee all that debt, because thou desiredst me. - **Matthew 18:32**
8. Shouldest not thou also have had compassion on thou fellow servant, even as I had pity on thee? - **Matthew 18:33**
9. And his lord was wroth, and delivered him to the tormentors, till he should pay all that was due unto him. - **Matthew 18:34**
10. So likewise shall my Heavenly Father do also unto you, if ye from your hearts forgive not everyone his brother their trespasses. - **Matthew 18:35**

February 1

JESUS SAID:

1. Have ye not read, that he which made them at the beginning made them male and female. - **Matthew 19:4**

2. And said, for this cause shall a man leave father and mother. - **Matthew 19:5**

3. And shall cleave to his wife. - **Matthew 19:5**

4. And they twain shall be one flesh. - **Matthew 19:5**

5. Wherefore they are no more twain, but one flesh. - **Matthew 19:6**

6. What therefore God has joined together, let not man put asunder. - **Matthew 19:6**

7. Moses, because of the hardness of your hearts suffered you to put away your wives. - **Matthew 19:8**

8. But from the beginning it was not so. - **Matthew 19:8**

9. And I say unto you whosoever shall put away his wife, except it be for fornication and shall marry another, committeth adultery. - **Matthew 19:9**

10. And whoso marrieth her which is put away doth commit adultery. - **Matthew 19:9**

February 2

JESUS SAID:

1. All men cannot receive this saying, save they to whom it is given. – **Matthew 19:11**

2. For there are some eunuchs, which were so born from their mother's wombs. – **Matthew 19:12**

3. And there are some eunuchs, which were made eunuchs of men. – **Matthew 19:12**

4. And there be eunuchs which have made themselves eunuchs for the kingdom of Heaven's sake. – **Matthew 19:12**

5. He that is able to receive it, let him receive it. – **Matthew 19:12**

6. Suffer little children and forbid them not, to come unto me. – **Matthew 19:14**

7. For of such is the kingdom of Heaven. – **Matthew 19:14**

8. Why callest thou me good? – **Matthew 19:17**

9. There is none good but one, that is, God. – **Matthew 19:17**

10. But if thou wilt enter into life, keep the commandments. – **Matthew 19:17**

February 3

JESUS SAID:

1. Thou shalt do no murder. - **Matthew 19:18**

2. Thou shalt not commit adultery. - **Matthew 19:18**

3. Thou shalt not steal. - **Matthew 19:18**

4. Thou shalt not bear false witness. - **Matthew 19:18**

5. Honor thy father and thy mother. - **Matthew 19:19**

6. Thou shalt love thy neighbor as thyself. - **Matthew 19:19**

7. If thou wilt be perfect, go and sell that thou hast and give to the poor. - **Matthew 19:21**

8. And thou shalt have treasure in Heaven. - **Matthew 19:21**

9. And come and follow me. - **Matthew 19:21**

10. Verily I say unto you, that a rich man shall hardly enter into the kingdom of Heaven. - **Matthew 19:23**

February 4

JESUS SAID:

1. And again I say unto you, it is easier for a camel to go through the eye of a needle, than for a rich man to enter into the kingdom of God. - **Matthew 19:24**

2. With men this is impossible, but with God all things are possible. - **Matthew 19:26**

3. Verily I say unto you, that ye which have followed me. - **Matthew 19:28**

4. In the regeneration when the Son of man shall sit in the throne of his glory. - **Matthew 19:28**

5. Ye also shall sit upon twelve thrones, judging the twelve tribes of Israel. - **Matthew 19:28**

6. And every one that has forsaken houses, or brethren or sisters, or father or mother, or wife, or children or lands for my name's sake! - **Matthew 19:29**

7. Shall receive hundredfold. - **Matthew 19:29**

8. And shall inherit everlasting life. - **Matthew 19:29**

9. But many that are first shall be last. - **Matthew 19:30**

10. And the last shall be first. - **Matthew 19:30**

February 5

JESUS SAID:

1. Behold, we go up to Jerusalem. - **Matthew 20:18**
2. And the Son of man shall be betrayed unto the chief priest and unto the scribes. – **Matthew 20:18**
3. And they shall condemn him to death. - **Matthew 20:18**
4. And shall deliver him to the Gentiles to mock, and to scourge and to crucify him. - **Matthew 20:19**
5. And the third day he shall rise again. - **Matthew 20:19**
6. What wilt thou? - **Matthew 20:21**
7. Ye know not what ye ask. - **Matthew 20:22**
8. Are ye able to drink of the cup that i shall drink of and to be baptized with the baptism that I am baptized with? - **Matthew 20:22**
9. Ye shall drink indeed of my cup and be baptized with the baptism that I am baptized with. - **Matthew 20:23**
10. But to sit on my right hand, and on my left, is not mine to give, but it shall be given to them for whom it is prepared of my Father. - **Matthew 20:23**

February 6

JESUS SAID:

1. Ye know that the princes of the Gentiles exercise dominion over them. - **Matthew 20:25**

2. And they that are great exercise authority upon them. - **Matthew 20:25**

3. But it shall not be so among you. - **Matthew 20:26**

4. But whosoever will be great among you, let him be your minister. - **Matthew 20:26**

5. And whosoever will be chief among you, let him be your servant. - **Matthew 20:27**

6. Even as the Son of man came not to be ministered unto, but to minister. - **Matthew 20:28**

7. And to give his life a ransom for many. - **Matthew 20:28**

8. What will ye, that I shall do unto you? - **Matthew 20:32**

9. Go into the village over against you, and straightway ye shall find an ass tied, and a colt with her; loose them, and bring them unto me. - **Matthew 21:2**

10. And if any man say ought unto you, ye shall say, the Lord hath need of them and straightway he will send them. - **Matthew 21:3**

February 7

JESUS SAID:

1. It is written my house shall be called the house of prayer.
   - **Matthew 21:13**

2. But ye have made it a den of thieves. - **Matthew 21:13**

3. Yea; have ye never read. - **Matthew 21:16**

4. Out of the mouth of babes and sucklings thou hast perfected praise. - **Matthew 21:16**

5. Let no fruit grow on thee henceforward forever.
   - **Matthew 21:19**

6. Verily I say unto you, if ye have faith. - **Matthew 21:21**

7. And doubt not. - **Matthew 21:21**

8. Ye shall not only do this which is done to the fig tree.
   - **Matthew 21:21**

9. But also if ye shall say, unto this mountain be thou removed, and be thou cast into the sea. - **Matthew 21:21**

10. It shall be done. - **Matthew 21:21**

February 8

JESUS SAID:

1. And all things whatsoever ye shall ask in prayer, believing, ye shall receive. - **Matthew 21:22**

2. I also will ask you one thing. - **Matthew 21:24**

3. Which if you tell me. - **Matthew 21:24**

4. I in likewise will tell you by what authority I do these things. - **Matthew 21:24**

5. The baptism of John, whence was it? - **Matthew 21:24**

6. From Heaven, or of men? - **Matthew 21:24**

7. Neither tell I you by what authority I do these things. - **Matthew 21:27**

8. But what think ye? - **Matthew 21:28**

9. A certain man had two sons. - **Matthew 21:28**

10. And he came to the first, and said, son go to work today in my vineyard. - **Matthew 21:28**

February 9

JESUS SAID:

1. He answered and said, I will not. - **Matthew 21:29**

2. But afterward he repented, and went. - **Matthew 21:29**

3. And he come to the second, and said likewise. - **Matthew 21:30**

4. And he answered and said, I go sir and went not. - **Matthew 21:30**

5. Whether of them twain did the will of his father. - **Matthew 21:31**

6. Verily I say unto you. - **Matthew 21:31**

7. That the publicans and the harlots go into the kingdom of God before you. - Matthew 21:31

8. For John came unto you in the way of righteousness. - **Matthew 21:32**

9. And ye believed him not. - **Matthew 21:32**

10. But the publicans and the harlots believed him, and ye, when ye had seen it, repented not afterwards, that ye might believe him. - **Matthew 21:32**

February 10

JESUS SAID:

1. Hear another parable there was a certain householder, which planted a vineyard. - **Matthew 21:33**

2. And hedged it round about, and digged a winepress in it. - **Matthew 21:33**

3. And built a tower. - **Matthew 21:33**

4. And let it out to husbandmen. - **Matthew 21:33**

5. And went into a far country. - **Matthew 21:33**

6. And when the time of the fruit drew near - **Matthew 21:33**

7. He sent his servants to the husbandmen. - **Matthew 21:34**

8. That they might receive the fruits of it. - **Matthew 21:34**

9. And the husbandmen took his servants, and beat one, and killed another, and stoned another. - **Matthew 21:35**

10. Again, he sent other servants more than the first! And they did unto them likewise. - **Matthew 21:36**

February 11

JESUS SAID:

1. But last of all he sent unto them his son saying, they will reverence my son. - **Matthew 21:37**

2. But when the husbandmen saw the son. - **Matthew 21:38**

3. They said among themselves, this is an heir, let us kill him, and let us siege on his inheritance. - **Matthew 21:38**

4. And they caught him and cast him out of the vineyard and slew him. - **Matthew 21:39**

5. When the Lord therefore of the vineyard cometh. - **Matthew 21:40**

6. What will he do unto those husbandmen? - **Matthew 21:40**

7. Did ye never read in the scripture. - **Matthew 21:42**

8. The stone which the builder rejected. - **Matthew 21:42**

9. The same is become the head of the corner. - **Matthew 21:42**

10. This is the Lord's doing and it is marvelous in our eyes? - **Matthew 21:42**

February 12
JESUS SAID:

1. Therefore say I unto you. - **Matthew 21:42**

2. The kingdom of God shall be taken from you, and given to a nation bringing forth the fruits thereof. - **Matthew 21:42**

3. And whosoever shall fall on this stone shall be broken. - **Matthew 21:44**

4. But on whomsoever it shall fall, it will grind him to powder. - **Matthew 21:44**

5. Why tempt me, ye hypocrites. - **Matthew 22:18**

6. Show me the tribute money. - **Matthew 22:19**

7. Whose is this image and superscription? - **Matthew 22:20**

8. Render therefore unto Caesar the things which are Caesar's and unto God the things that are God's. - **Matthew 22:21**

9. Ye do err, not knowing the scripture. - **Matthew 22:29**

10. Nor the power of God. - **Matthew 22:29**

February 13

JESUS SAID:

1. For in the resurrection they neither marry, nor are given in marriage, but are as the angels of God in Heaven.
   - **Matthew 22:30**

2. But as touching the resurrection of the dead, have ye not read that which was spoken unto you, by God, saying. - **Matthew 22:31**

3. I am the God of Abraham, and the God of Isaac, and the God of Jacob? - **Matthew 22:33**

4. God is not the God of the dead, but of the living.
   - **Matthew 22:32**

5. Thou shalt love the Lord thy God with all thy heart.
   - **Matthew 22:37**

6. And with all thy soul. - **Matthew 22:37**

7. And with all thy mind. - **Matthew 22:37**

8. This is the first and great commandment. - **Matthew 22:38**

9. And the second is like unto it, thou shalt love thy neighbor as thyself. - **Matthew 22:39**

10. On these two commandments hang all the law and the prophets. - **Matthew 22:40**

February 14

JESUS SAID:

1. What think ye of the Christ? - **Matthew 22:42**

2. Whose son is he? - **Matthew 22:42**

3. How then doth David in spirit call him Lord? Saying, the Lord said unto my Lord, sit thou on my right hand, till I make thine enemies thy footstool? - **Matthew 22:43-44**

4. If David then called him Lord, how is he his son? - **Matthew 22:45**

5. The scribes and the Pharisees sit in Moses seat. - **Matthew 23:2**

6. All therefore whatsoever they bid you observe. - **Matthew 23:3**

7. That observe and do. - **Matthew 23:3**

8. But do not ye after their works, for they say and do not. - **Matthew 23:3**

9. For they bind heavy burdens and grievous to be born, and lay them on men shoulder. - **Matthew 23:4**

10. But they themselves will not move them with one of their fingers. - **Matthew 23:4**

February 15

JESUS SAID:

1. But all their works they do for to be seen of men. - **Matthew 23:5**

2. They make broad their phylacteries. - **Matthew 23:5**

3. And enlarge the borders of their garments. - **Matthew 23:5**

4. And love the uppermost rooms at feasts, and the chief seats in the synagogues. - **Matthew 23:6**

5. And greetings in the markets, and to be called of men Rabbi, Rabbi. - **Matthew 23:8**

6. But be not ye called Rabbi: - **Matthew 23:8**

7. For one is your Master. - **Matthew 23:8**

8. Even Christ. - **Matthew 23:8**

9. And all ye are brethren. - **Matthew 23:8**

10. And call no man your father upon the earth; for one is your Father, which is in Heaven. - **Matthew 23:9**

February 16

JESUS SAID:

1. Neither be ye called master, for one is your Master, even Christ. - **Matthew 23:10**

2. But he that is greatest among you shall be your servant. - **Matthew 23:11**

3. And whosoever shall exalt himself shall be abased. - **Matthew 23:12**

4. And he that shall humble himself shall be exalted. - **Matthew 23:12**

5. But woe unto you scribes and Pharisees, hypocrites. - **Matthew 23:13**

6. For ye shut up the kingdom of Heaven against men. - **Matthew 23:13**

7. For ye neither go in yourselves, neither suffer ye them that are entering to go in. - **Matthew 23:13**

8. Woe to you, scribes and Pharisees, hypocrites, for ye devour widows' houses, and for a pretence make long prayer. - **Matthew 23:14**

9. Therefore ye shall receive the greater damnation. - **Matthew 23:14**

10. Woe to you scribes, and Pharisees, hypocrites! For you compass sea and land to make one proselyte, and when he is made, ye make him twofold more the child of hell than yourselves. - **Matthew 23:15**

February 17

JESUS SAID:

1. Woe unto you, ye blind guides, which say, whosoever shall swear by the temple, it is nothing, but whosoever shall swear by the gold of the temple he is a debtor. - **Matthew 23:16**
2. Jesus said ye fools and blind; for whether is greater, the gold, or the temple that sanctified the gold. - **Matthew 23:17**
3. And whosoever shall swear by the altar, it is nothing; but whosoever sweareth by the gift that is upon it, he is guilty. - **Matthew 23:18**
4. Ye fools and blind; for whether is greater, the gift, or the altar that sanctifieth the gift? - **Matthew 23:19**
5. Whoso therefore shall swear by the altar, sweareth by it, and by all things thereon. - **Matthew 23:20**
6. And whoso shall swear by the temple, sweareth by it, and him that dwelleth therein. - **Matthew 23:21**
7. And he that shall swear by Heaven, sweareth by the throne of God, and by him that sitteth thereon. - **Matthew 23:22**
8. Woe unto you, scribes and Pharisees, hypocrites. - **Matthew 23:23**
9. For ye pay tithe of mint and anise and cummin and have omitted the weightier matters of the law, judgement, mercy, and faith. - **Matthew 23:23**
10. These ought ye to have done, and not to leave the other undone. - **Matthew 23:23**

February 18

JESUS SAID:

1. Ye blind guides, which strain at a gnat, and swallow a camel.
   - **Matthew 23:24**
2. Woe to you, scribes and Pharisees, hypocrites!
   - **Matthew 23:25**
3. For you made clean the outside of a cup, and the platter, but within, they are full of extortion and excess. - **Matthew 23:25**
4. Thou blind Pharisee cleanse first that which is within the cup and platter, that the outside of them may be clean also.
   - **Matthew 23:26**
5. Woe to you, scribes and Pharisees, hypocrites! For ye are like unto whited sepulchres, which indeed appear beautiful outward, but are within full of dead men's bones, and of all uncleanness. - **Matthew 23:27**
6. Even so ye also outwardly appear righteous unto men.
   - **Matthew 23:28**
7. But within ye are full of hypocrisy and iniquity.
   - **Matthew 23:28**
8. Woe unto you, scribes and Pharisees, hypocrites! Because you build the tombs of the prophets, and garnish the sepulchres of the righteous. - **Matthew 23:29**
9. And say, if we had been in the days of our father, we would not have been partakers with them in the blood of the prophets. - **Matthew 23:30**
10. Wherefore ye be witnesses unto yourselves, that ye are the children of them which killed the prophets. - **Matthew 23:31**

February 19

JESUS SAID:

1. *Fill ye up then the measure of your fathers.* - **Matthew 23:32**

2. *Ye serpents, ye generation of vipers, how can ye escape the damnation of hell?* - **Matthew 23:33**

3. *Wherefore, behold I send unto you prophets, and wise men and scribes.* - **Matthew 23:34**

4. *And some of them ye shall kill and crucify.* - **Matthew 23:34**

5. *And some of them shall ye scourge in your synagogues and persecute them from city to city.* - **Matthew 23:34**

6. *That upon you may come all the righteous blood shed upon the earth.* - **Matthew 23:35**

7. *From the blood of righteous Abel unto the blood of Zacharias son of Barachias whom you slew between the temple and the altar.* - **Matthew 23:35**

8. *Verily I say unto you, all these things shall come upon this generation.* - **Matthew 23:36**

9. *O Jerusalem, Jerusalem, thou that killest the prophets, and stonest them which are sent unto thee.* - **Matthew 23:37**

10. *How often would I have gathered thy children together, even as a hen gathereth her chickens under her wings, and ye would not!* - **Matthew 23:37**

February 20
JESUS SAID:

1. Behold, your house is left unto you desolate. - **Matthew 23:38**

2. But I say unto you, ye shall not see me henceforth till ye shall say. Blessed is he that cometh in the name of the Lord. - **Matthew 23:39**

3. See ye not all these things? - **Matthew 24:2**

4. Verily I say unto you, there shall not be left here one stone upon another, that shall not be thrown down. - **Matthew 24:2**

5. Take heed that no man deceive you. - **Matthew 24:4**

6. For many shall come in my name, saying, I am Christ and shall deceive many. - **Matthew 24:5**

7. And ye shall hear of wars and rumors of wars. - **Matthew 24:6**

8. See that ye be not troubled. - **Matthew 24:6**

9. For all these things must come to pass. - **Matthew 24:6**

10. But the end is not yet. - **Matthew 24:6**

February 21

JESUS SAID:

1. For nation shall rise against nation. - **Matthew 24:7**

2. And kingdom against kingdom. - **Matthew 24:7**

3. And there shall be famines, and pestilences, and earthquakes, in divers places. - **Matthew 24:7**

4. All these are the beginning of sorrows. - **Matthew 24:8**

5. Then shall they deliver you up to be afflicted. - **Matthew 24:9**

6. And shall kill you. - **Matthew 24:9**

7. And ye shall be hated of all nations for my name's sake. - **Matthew 24:9**

8. And then shall many be offended. -**Matthew 24:10**

9. And shall betray one another, and shall hate one another. - **Matthew 24:10**

10. And many false prophets shall rise, and shall deceive many. - **Matthew 24:11**

February 22

JESUS SAID:

1. And because iniquity shall abound, the love of many shall wax cold. - **Matthew 24:12**

2. But he that endures until the end, the same shall be saved. - **Matthew 24:13**

3. And this gospel of the kingdom shall be preached in all the world for a witness unto all nations. - **Matthew 24:14**

4. And then shall the end come. - **Matthew 24:14**

5. When ye therefore shall see the abomination of desolation, spoken of by Daniel the prophet stand in the holy place. - **Matthew 24:15**

6. Then let them which be in Judaea flee into the mountains. - **Matthew 24:16**

7. Let him which is on the housetop not come down to take anything out of his house. - **Matthew 24:17**

8. Neither let him which in the field return back to take his clothes. - **Matthew 24:18**

9. And woe unto them that are with child and to them that give suck in those days. - **Matthew 24:19**

10. But pray ye that your flight be not in the winter, neither on the Sabbath day. - **Matthew 24:20**

February 23

JESUS SAID:

1. For then shall be great tribulation, such as was not since the beginning of the world to this time. - **Matthew 24:21**

2. No, nor ever shall be. - **Matthew 24:21**

3. And except those days should be shortened, there should no flesh be saved. - **Matthew 24:22**

4. But for the elect's sake those days shall be shortened. - **Matthew 24:22**

5. Then if any man shall say unto you, lo here's Christ, or there, believe it not. - **Matthew 24:23**

6. For there shall arise false Christs and false prophets, and shall shew great signs and wonders. - **Matthew 24:21**

7. Insomuch that, if it were possible, they shall deceive the very elect. - **Matthew 24:24**

8. Behold, I have told you before. - **Matthew 24:25**

9. Wherefore if they say unto you, behold he is in the desert, go not forth; behold, he is in the secret chambers; believe it not. - **Matthew 24:26**

10. For as the lightning cometh out of the east and shineth even to the west; so shall also the coming of the Son of man be. - **Matthew 24:27**

February 24

JESUS SAID:

1. For wheresoever the carcass is there will the eagles be gathered together. -**Matthew 24:28**

2. Immediately after the tribulation of those days shall the sun be darkened, and the moon shall not give her light.
– **Matthew 24:29**

3. And the stars shall fall from Heaven. – **Matthew 24:29**

4. And the power of the Heavens shall be shaken.
– **Matthew 24:29**

5. And then shall appear the sign of the Son of man in Heaven.
– **Matthew 24:30**

6. And then shall all the tribes of the earth mourn.
– **Matthew 24:30**

7. And they shall see the Son of man coming in the clouds of Heaven with power and great glory. – **Matthew 24:30**

8. And he shall send his angels with a great sound of a trumpet.
– **Matthew 24:31**

9. And they shall gather together his elect from the four winds.
– **Matthew 24:31**

10. From one end of Heaven to the other. – **Matthew 24:31**

February 25

JESUS SAID:

1. Now learn a parable of the fig tree. - **Matthew 24:32**
2. When its branch is yet tender and putteth forth leaves, ye know that summer is nigh. - **Matthew 24:32**
3. So likewise, when ye shall see all these things, know that it is near. - **Matthew 24:33**
4. Even at the door. - **Matthew 24:33**
5. Verily I say unto you. - **Matthew 24:34**
6. This generation shall not pass, till all these things be fulfilled. - **Matthew 24:34**
7. Heaven & earth shall pass away but my words shall not pass away. - **Matthew 24:35**
8. But of that day and hour knoweth no man. - **Matthew 24:36**
9. No, not the angels of Heaven, but my Father only. - **Matthew 24:36**
10. But as the days of Noah were, so shall also the coming of the Son of man be. - **Matthew 24:37**

February 26

JESUS SAID:

1. For as in the days that were before the flood they were eating and drinking, marrying and giving in marriage.
   - **Matthew 24:38**

2. Until the day that Noah entered into the ark.
   - **Matthew 24:38**

3. And knew not until the flood came, and took them all away.
   - **Matthew 24:39**

4. So shall also the coming of the Son of man be.
   - **Matthew 24:39**

5. Then shall two be in the field. - **Matthew 24:40**

6. The one shall be taken, and the other left. - **Matthew 24:40**

7. Two women shall be grinding at the mill. - **Matthew 24:41**

8. The one shall be taken and the other left. - **Matthew 24:41**

9. Watch therefore; for ye know not what hour your Lord doth come. - **Matthew 24:42**

10. But know this, that if the goodman of the house had known in what watch the thief would come he would have watched, and would not have suffered his house to be broken up.
    - **Matthew 24:43**

February 27

JESUS SAID:

1. Therefore be ye also ready. - **Matthew 24:44**

2. For in such an hour as ye think not the Son of man cometh. - **Matthew 24:44**

3. Who then is a faithful and wise servant, whom his Lord hath made ruler over his household. - **Matthew 24:45**

4. To give them meat in due season? - **Matthew 24:45**

5. Blessed is that servant, whom his Lord when he cometh shall find so doing. - **Matthew 24:46**

6. Verily, I say unto you, that he shall make him ruler over all his goods. - **Matthew 24:47**

7. But if that evil servant shall say in his heart my Lord delayeth his coming. - **Matthew 24:48**

8. And shall begin the smite his fellow servants and to eat and drink with the drunken. - **Matthew 24:49**

9. The Lord of that servant shall come in a day when he looketh not for him, and in an hour that he is not aware of. - **Matthew 24:50**

10. And shall cut him asunder, and appoint him his portion with the hypocrites, there shall be weeping and gnashing of teeth. - **Matthew 24:51**

February 28

JESUS SAID:

1. Then shall the kingdom of Heaven be likened unto ten virgins. - **Matthew 25:1**

2. Which took their lamps and went forth to meet the bridegroom. - **Matthew 25:1**

3. And five of them were wise. - **Matthew 25:2**

4. And five were foolish. - **Matthew 25:2**

5. They that were foolish took their lamps, and took no oil with them. - **Matthew 25:3**

6. But the wise took oil in their vessels with their lamps. - **Matthew 25:4**

7. While the bridegroom tarried, they all slumbered and slept. - **Matthew 25:5**

8. And at midnight there was a cry made. - **Matthew 25:6**

9. Behold, the bridegroom cometh. - **Matthew 25:6**

10. Go ye out to meet him. - **Matthew 25:6**

February 29

JESUS SAID:

1. Then all those virgins arose and trimmed their lamps.
   - **Matthew 25:7**

2. And the foolish said unto the wise, give us of your oil, for our lamps are gone out. - **Matthew 25:8**

3. But the wise answered saying, not so, lest there be not enough for us and you, but go ye rather to them that sell, and buy for yourselves. - **Matthew 25:9**

4. And while they went to buy, the bridegroom came.
   - **Matthew 25:10**

5. And they that were ready went in with him to the marriage.
   - **Matthew 25:10**

6. And the door was shut. - **Matthew 25:10**

7. Afterwards came also the other virgins, saying Lord, Lord, open to us. - **Matthew 25:11**

8. But he answered and said, verily i say unto you I know you not. - **Matthew 25:12**

9. Watch therefore. - **Matthew 25:13**

10. For ye know neither the day nor the hour wherein the Son of man cometh. – **Matthew 25:13**

March 1

JESUS SAID:

1. For the kingdom of Heaven is as a man traveling into a far country. - **Matthew 25:14**

2. Who called his own servants, and delivered unto them his goods. - **Matthew 25:14**

3. And unto one he gave five talents. - **Matthew 25:15**

4. To another two. - **Matthew 25:15**

5. And to another one. - **Matthew 25:15**

6. To every man to his several ability. - **Matthew 25:15**

7. And straightway took his journey. - **Matthew 25:15**

8. Then he that had received the five talents went and traded with the same, and made them other five talents. - **Matthew 25:16**

9. And likewise he that had received two he also gained other two. - **Matthew 25:17**

10. But he that had received one, went and digged in the earth, and hid his Lord's money. - **Matthew 25:18**

March 2

JESUS SAID:

1. After a long time the Lord of those servants cometh, and reckoned with them. – **Matthew 25:19**

2. And so he that received five talents came and brought other five talents. - **Matthew 25:20**

3. Saying Lord thou deliveredst unto me five talents, I have gained beside them five talents more. - **Matthew 25:20**

4. His Lord said to him, thou good and faithful servant, thou hast been faithful over a few things. I will make thee ruler over many things, enter thou into the joy of thy Lord. – **Matthew 25:21**

5. He also that had received two talents came and said, Lord, thou deliveredst unto me two talents, behold, I have gained two other talents besides them. - **Matthew 25:22**

6. His Lord said unto him well done, good and faithful servant, thou hast been faithful over a few things, I will make thee ruler over many things; enter now into the joy of thy Lord. – **Matthew 25:23**

7. Then he which had received the one talent came and said, Lord, I knew then that thou art an hard man, reaping when thou hast not sown, and gathering where thou hast not strawed, and I was afraid, and went and hid thy talent in the earth, lo there thou hast that is thine. - **Matthew 25:24**

8. His Lord answered and said unto him. Thou wicked and slothful servant, thou knewest that I reap here I sowed not and gathered where I have not strawed. Thou oughtest therefore to have put my money to the exchanges and then at my coming I should have received my own with usury. Take therefore the talent from him and give it to him that has ten talents - **Matthew 25:26**-28.

9. For unto every one that hath shall be given, and he shall have abundance. - **Matthew 25:29**

10. But from him that hath not shall be taken away even that which he hath. -**Matthew 25:29**

March 3

JESUS SAID:

1. And cast ye the unprofitable servant into outer darkness.
   - **Matthew 25:30**

2. There shall be weeping and gnashing of teeth.
   - **Matthew 25:30**

3. When the Son of man shall come in this glory, and all the holy angels with him, then shall he sit upon the throne of his glory. - **Matthew 25:31**

4. And before him shall be gathered all nations, and he shall separate them one from another. - **Matthew 25:32**

5. As a shepherd divideth his sheep from the goat.
   - **Matthew 25:32**

6. And he shall set the sheep on his right hand. - **Matthew 25:33**

7. But the goats on the left. - **Matthew 25:33**

8. Then shall the King say unto them on his right-hand, come, ye blessed of my Father. - **Matthew 25:34**

9. Inherit the kingdom. - **Matthew 25:34**

10. Prepared for you from the foundation of the world.
    - **Matthew 25:34**

March 4

JESUS SAID:

1. For I was an hungred, and ye gave me meat. - **Matthew 25:35**

2. I was thirsty, and ye gave me drink. - **Matthew 25:35**

3. I was a stranger and ye took me in. - **Matthew 25:35**

4. Naked, and ye clothed me. - **Matthew 25:36**

5. I was sick and ye visited me. - **Matthew 25:36**

6. I was in prison and ye came unto me. - **Matthew 25:36**

7. Then shall the righteous answer him, saying, Lord, when saw we thee an hungred, and fed thee? When saw we thee a stranger, and took thee in or naked and clothed thee? Or when saw we thee sick, or in prison, and came unto thee? - **Matthew 25:37-39**

8. And the King shall answer and say unto them verily I say unto you. - **Matthew 25:40**

9. Inasmuch as ye have done it unto one of the least of these my brethren, ye have done it unto me. - **Matthew 25:40**

10. Then shall he say also unto them on the left hand. Depart from me, ye cursed, into everlasting fire, prepared for the devil and his angels. - **Matthew 25:41**

March 5

JESUS SAID:

1. For I was hungered and ye gave me no meat. - **Matthew 25:42**

2. I was thirsty and ye gave me no drink. - **Matthew 25:42**

3. I was a stranger and ye took me not in. - **Matthew 25:43**

4. Naked, and you clothed me not. - **Matthew 25:43**

5. Sick and in prison, and ye visited me not. - **Matthew 25:43**

6. Then shall they also answer him saying, Lord when saw we thee hungered, or athirst, or a stranger, or naked, or sick, or in prison, and did not minister unto thee. - **Matthew 25:44**

7. Then shall he answer them saying, verily I say unto you. - **Matthew 25:45**

8. Inasmuch as ye did it not to one of the least of these, ye did it not to me. - **Matthew 25:45**

9. And these shall go away into everlasting punishment. - **Matthew 25:46**

10. But the righteous into eternal life. - **Matthew 25:46**

March 6

JESUS SAID:

1. Ye know that after two days is the feast of the Passover.
   - **Matthew 26:2**

2. And the Son of man is betrayed to be crucified.
   - **Matthew 26:2**

3. Why trouble ye the woman for she hath wrought a good work upon me. - **Matthew 26:10**

4. For ye have the poor always with you. - **Matthew 26:11**

5. But me ye have not always. - **Matthew 26:11**

6. For in that she hath poured this ointment on my body she did it for my burial. - **Matthew 26:12**

7. Verily I say unto you. - **Matthew 26:13**

8. Wheresoever the gospel shall be preached in the whole world.
   - **Matthew 26:13**

9. There shall also this that this woman hath done.
   - **Matthew 26:13**

10. Be told for a memorial of her. - **Matthew 26:13**

March 7

JESUS SAID:

1. Go into the city to such a man, and say unto him, the Master saith, my time is at hand. - **Matthew 26:18**

2. I will keep the Passover at thy house with my disciples. - **Matthew 26:18**

3. Verily I say unto you, that one of you shall betray me. - **Matthew 26:21**

4. The Son of man goeth as it is written of him. - **Matthew 26:24**

5. But woe unto that man by whom the Son of man is betrayed. - **Matthew 26:24**

6. It had been good for that man if he had not been born. - **Matthew 26:24**

7. Thou hast said. - **Matthew 26:25**

8. Take, eat, this is my body. - **Matthew 26:26**

9. Drink ye all of it. - **Matthew 26:27**

10. For this is my blood of the new testament, which is shed for many for the remission of sins. - **Matthew 26:28**

March 8

JESUS SAID:

1. But I say unto you, I will not drink henceforth of this fruit of the vine until that day when I drink it new with you in my Father's kingdom. - **Matthew 26:29**

2. All ye shall be offended because of me this night. |- **Matthew 26:31**

3. For it is written, I will smite the Shepherd, and the sheep of the flock shall be scattered abroad. - **Matthew 26:31**

4. But after I am risen again. - **Matthew 26:32**

5. I will go before you into Galilee. - **Matthew 26:32**

6. Verily, I say unto thee. - **Matthew 26:34**

7. That this night before the cock crows, thou shalt deny me thrice. - **Matthew 26:34**

8. Sit ye here, while I go and pray yonder. - **Matthew 26:36**

9. My soul is exceeding sorrowful, even unto death. - **Matthew 26:38**

10. Tarry ye here, and watch with me. - **Matthew 26:38**

March 9

JESUS SAID:

1. O, my Father, if it be possible, let this cup pass from me.
   - **Matthew 26:39**

2. Nevertheless, not as I will, but as thou wilt. - **Matthew 26:39**

3. What, could ye not watch with me one hour?
   - **Matthew 26:40**

4. Watch and pray, that ye enter not into temptation.
   - **Matthew 26:41**

5. The spirit indeed is willing, but the flesh is weak.
   - **Matthew 26:41**

6. O my Father, if this cup may not pass away from me, except I drink it, thy will be done. - **Matthew 26:42**

7. Sleep on now, and take your rest. - **Matthew 26:45**

8. Behold the hour is at hand, and the Son of man is betrayed into the hands of sinners. - **Matthew 26:45**

9. Rise, let us be going. - **Matthew 26:46**

10. Behold, he is at hand that doth betray me. - **Matthew 26:46**

March 10

JESUS SAID:

1. Friend, wherefore art thou come?- **Matthew 26:50**

2. Put up again thy sword into his place. - **Matthew 26:52**

3. For all they that take the sword shall perish with the sword. - **Matthew 26:52**

4. Thinkest thou that I cannot now pray to my Father, and he shall presently give me more than twelve legions of angels? - **Matthew 26:53**

5. But how then shall the scriptures be fulfilled. - **Matthew 26:54**

6. That thus it must be. - **Matthew 26:54**

7. Are ye come out as against a thief with swords and staves for to take me? - **Matthew 26:55**

8. I sat daily with you teaching in the temple. - **Matthew 26:55**

9. And ye laid no hold on me! - **Matthew 26:55**

10. But all this was done that the scriptures of the prophets might be fulfilled. – **Matthew 26:56**

March 11

JESUS SAID:

1. Thou hast said. - **Matthew 26:64**

2. Nevertheless I say unto you. - **Matthew 26:64**

3. Hereafter shall ye see the Son of man sitting on the right hand of power, and coming in the clouds of Heaven.
   - **Matthew 26:64**

4. Before the cock crow, thou shalt deny me thrice.
   - **Matthew 26:75**

5. Eli, Eli, la-ma sa-bach-tha-ni? My God, my God, why hast thou forsaken me? - **Matthew 27:46**

6. After three days I will rise again. - **Matthew 27:63**

7. All hail. - **Matthew 28:9**

8. Be not afraid. - **Matthew 28:10**

9. Go tell my brethren that they go into Galilee and there shall they see me. - **Matthew 28:10**

10. All power is given unto me in Heaven and in earth.
    - **Matthew 28:18**

March 12

JESUS SAID:

1. Go ye therefore and teach all nations. - **Matthew 28:19**

2. Baptizing them in the name of the Father, and the Son, and of the Holy Ghost. - **Matthew 28:19**

3. Teaching them to observe all things whatsoever I have commanded you. - **Matthew 28:20**

4. And, lo, I am with you always, even unto the end of the world. - **Matthew 28:20**

5. Amen. - **Matthew 28:20**

6. Go ye unto all the world, and preach the gospel to every creature. - **Mark 16:15**

7. He that believeth and is baptized shall be saved. - **Mark 16:16**

8. But he that believeth not shall be damned. - **Mark 16:16**

9. And these signs shall follow them that believe. - **Mark 16:17**

10. In my name shall they cast out devils; they shall speak with new tongues. - **Mark 16:17**

March 13

JESUS SAID:

1. They shall take up serpents. – **Mark 16:18**

2. And if they drink any deadly thing, it shall not hurt them. – **Mark 16:18**

3. They shall lay hands on the sick, and they shall recover. – **Mark 16:18**

4. These are the words which I spake unto you while I was yet with you. – **Luke 24:44**

5. That all things must be fulfilled, which were written in the law of Moses, and in the prophets, and in the psalms concerning me. – **Luke 24:44**

6. Thus it is written and it behooved Christ to suffer. – **Luke 24:46**

7. And to rise from the dead the third day. – **Luke 24:46**

8. And that repentance and remission of sins should be preached in his name among all nations beginning in Jerusalem. – **Luke 24:47**

9. And ye are witnesses of these things. – **Luke 24:48**

10. And behold, I send the promise of my Father upon you, but tarry ye in the city of Jerusalem, until ye be endued with power from on high. – **Luke 24:49**

March 14

JESUS SAID:

1. I have overcome the world. - **John 16:33**

2. Be of good cheer. - **John 16:33**

3. I will see you again. - **John 16:22**

4. Your heart shall rejoice. - **John 16:22**

5. Your joy no man taketh from you. - **John 16:22**

6. All power is given unto me on earth. - **Matthew 28:18**

7. And whatsoever ye shall ask in my name, that I will do, that the Father may be glorified in the Son. - **John 14:13**

8. If you love me, keep my commandments. - **John 14:15**

9. The Comforter (Holy Ghost) shall teach you all things and bring to you remembrance all things of me that I have said or taught. - **John 14:26**

10. If ye ask anything in my name, I will do it. - **John 14:13**

March 15

JESUS SAID:

1. Ask, and it shall be given. - **Matthew 7:7**

2. Seek and ye shall find. - **Matthew 7:7**

3. Knock, and it shall be opened unto you. - **Matthew 7:7**

4. If ye, then being evil, know how to give good gifts unto your children. - **Luke 11:13**

5. How much more shall your Heavenly Father give the Holy Spirit to them that ask him. - **Luke 11:13**

6. But the Comforter, which is the Holy Ghost, whom the Father will send in my name. - **John 14:26**

7. He shall teach you all things. - **John 14:26**

8. And bring all things to your remembrance, whatsoever I have said unto you. - **John 14:26**

9. Your sorrow shall be turned into joy. - **John 16:20**

10. That they all may be one: as thou, Father, art in me, and I in thee, that they also may be one in us. - **John 17:21**

March 16

JESUS SAID:

1. Peace I leave with you, my peace I give unto you. - **John 14:27**

2. Come unto me, all ye that labour and are heavy laden and I will give you rest. - **Matthew 11:28**

3. This day is salvation, come to this house, for so much as he also is a son of Abraham. For the Son of man is come to seek and to save that which was lost. - **Luke 19:9-10**

4. And I will pray the Father, and he shall give you another comforter, that may abide with you forever. - **John 14:16**

5. Even the spirit of truth, whom the world cannot receive, because it seeth him not, neither knoweth him but ye know him, for he dwelleth with you, and shall be in you. - **John 14:17**

6. Verily I say unto you, all sins shall be forgiven unto the sons of men. - **Mark 3:28**

7. I am with you always, even unto the end of the world. - **Matthew 28:20**

8. Therefore I say unto you take no thought for your life, what ye shall eat, or what ye shall drink. - **Matthew 6:25**

9. Nor yet for your body, what ye shall put on. - **Matthew 6:25**

10. Is not your life more that meat? - **Matthew 6:25**

March 17

JESUS SAID:

1. Is not your body more than raiment? - **Matthew 6:25**
2. Take no thought of the morrow for sufficient unto the day is the evil thereof. - **Matthew 6:34**
3. Verily I say unto you, all sins shall be forgiven unto the sons of men. - **Mark 3:28**
4. And I say unto you, ask and it shall be given. - **Luke 11:9**
5. I will come and heal him. - **Matthew 8:7**
6. Take therefore no thought for tomorrow,for the morrow shall take thought for the things of itself - **Matthew 6:34**
7. Do not be afraid. - **Mark 5:36**
8. Peace I leave with you, my peace I give unto you. - **John 14:27**
9. At that day ye shall know that I am in my Father, and ye in me, and I in you. - **John 14:20**
10. For God so loved the world, that he gave his only begotten Son, that whosoever believeth in him should not perish, but have everlasting life. - **John 3:16**

March 18

JESUS SAID:

1. He that believeth not in me is condemned. - **John 3:18**

2. If thou knewest the gift of God, and who it is that saith to thee, give me to drink; thou wouldest have asked of him, and he would have given thee living water. - **John 4:10**

3. I am the living bread which came down from Heaven, if any man eat of this bread he shall live forever. - **John 6:51**

4. I am the light of the world, he that followeth me shall not walk in darkness, but shall have the light of life. - **John 8:12**

5. Come to me that you may have life. - **John 10:10**

6. How can ye believe, which receive honor one of another, and seek not the honor that cometh from God only? - **John 5:44**

7. But if ye believe not Moses writings, how shall ye believe my words. - **John 5:47**

8. These things I have spoken unto you, that in me ye might have peace. - **John 16:33**

9. In the world ye shall have tribulations, but be of good cheer, I have overcome the world. - **John 16:33**

10. Sanctify them through thy truth; thy word is truth. - **John 17:17**

March 19

JESUS SAID:

1. O' thou of little faith wherefore didst thou doubt.
   - **Matthew 14:31**

2. Let not your heart be troubled. - **John 14:27**

3. I and my Father are one. - **John 10:30**

4. The works that I do in my Father's name; they bear witness of me. - **John 10:25**

5. All things have been committed to me by my Father.
   - **Matthew 11:27**

6. I am the good shepherd, the good shepherd giveth his life for the sheep. - **John 10:11**

7. Follow me. - **John 21:19, 22**

8. Blessed is he, whosoever shall not be offended in me.
   - **Matthew 11:6**

9. All power is given me in Heaven and on earth.
   - **Matthew 28:18**

10. But the hour cometh, and now is when the true worshippers shall worship the Father in spirit and in truth. - **John 4:23**

March 20

JESUS SAID:

1. The Father seeketh such to worship him, God is a Spirit and they that worship him must worship him in spirit and truth. – **John 4:23-24**

2. Come to me all ye that labour and are heavy laden, and I will give you rest. – **Matthew 11:28**

3. Murmur not among yourselves. – **John 6:43**

4. Verily, verily, I say unto you, that there be some of them that stand here. – **Mark 9:1**

5. Which shall not taste of death. – **Mark 9:1**

6. Till they have seen the kingdom of God come with power. – **Mark 9:1**

7. Elias verily cometh first. – **Mark 9:12**

8. And restoreth all things. – **Mark 9:12**

9. And how it is written of the Son of man, that he must suffer many things, and be set at nought. – **Mark 9:12**

10. But I say unto you, that Elias is indeed come, and they have done unto him whatsoever they listed, as it is written of him. – **Mark 9:13**

March 21

JESUS SAID:

1. What question ye with them? - **Mark 9:16**

2. O faithless generation,how long shall i be with you, how long shall I suffer you? - **Mark 9:19**

3. Jesus said bring him unto me. - **Mark 9:19**

4. How long is it ago since this came unto him? - **Mark 9:21**

5. If thou canst believe, all things are possible to him that believeth. - **Mark 9:23**

6. Thou dumb and deaf spirit, I charge thee, come out of him. - **Mark 9:25**

7. And enter no more into him. - **Mark 9:25**

8. This kind can come forth by nothing but by prayer and fasting. - **Mark 9:29**

9. The Son of man is delivered into the hands of men. - **Mark 9:31**

10. And they shall kill him, an after he is killed, he shall rise the third day. - **Mark 9:31**

March 22

JESUS SAID:

1. What was it that ye disputed among yourselves by the way? - **Mark 9:33**

2. If any man desire to be first, the same shall be last of all, and servant of all. - **Mark 9:35**

3. Whosoever shall receive one of such children in my name, receiveth me. - **Mark 9:37**

4. And whosoever receiveth me, receiveth not me but him that sent me. - **Mark 9:37**

5. Forbid him not, for there is no man which shall do a miracle in my name, that can lightly speak evil of me. - **Mark 9:39**

6. For he that is not against us is on our part. - **Mark 9:40**

7. For whosoever shall give you a cup of water to drink in my name, because ye belong to Christ. - **Mark 9:41**

8. Verily I say unto you he shall not lose his reward. - **Mark 9:41**

9. And whosoever shall offend one of these little ones that believe in me. - **Mark 9:42**

10. It is better for him that a millstone were hanged around his neck, and he were cast into the sea. - **Mark 9:42**

March 23

JESUS SAID:

1. And if thy hand offend thee, cut it off. - **Mark 9:43**
2. It is better for thee to enter into life maimed than to have two hands and go to hell. - **Mark 9:43**
3. Into the fire that never shall be quenched. - **Mark 9:43**
4. Where their worm dieth not. - **Mark 9:44**
5. And the fire is not quenched. - **Mark 9:44**
6. And if thy foot offend thee, cut it off. - **Mark 9:45**
7. It is better for thee to enter halt into life, than having two feet to be cast into hell. - **Mark 9:45**
8. Into the fire that never shall be quenched. - **Mark 9:45**
9. Where their worm dieth not. - **Mark 9:46**
10. And the fire is not quenched. - **Mark 9:46**

March 24

JESUS SAID:

1. And if thine eye offend thee, pluck it out. - **Mark 9:47**
2. It is better for thee to enter into the kingdom of God with one eye, than having two eyes to be cast into hell fire. - **Mark 9:48**
3. Where their worm dieth not. - **Mark 9:48**
4. And the fire is not quenched. - **Mark 9:48**
5. For every one shall be salted with fire. - **Mark 9:49**
6. And every sacrifice shall be salted with salt. - **Mark 9:49**
7. Salt is good, but if the salt have lost his saltness. - **Mark 9:50**
8. Wherewith will ye season it. - **Mark 9:50**
9. Have salt in yourselves. - **Mark 9:50**
10. And have peace one with another. - **Mark 9:50**

March 25

JESUS SAID:

1. What did Moses command you? - **Mark 10:3**

2. For the hardness of your heart, he wrote you this precept - **Mark 10:5**

3. But from the beginning of creation God made them male and female. **Mark 10:6**

4. For this cause shall a man leave his father and mother, and cleave to his wife. - **Mark 10:7**

5. And they twain shall be one flesh. - **Mark 10:8**

6. So then they are no more twain, but one flesh. - **Mark 10:8**

7. What therefore God hath joined together. - **Mark 10:9**

8. Let not man put asunder. - **Mark 10:9**

9. Whosoever shall put away his wife, and marry another, committeth adultery against her. - **Mark 10:11**

10. And if a woman shall put away her husband, and be married to another, she committeth adultery. - **Mark 10:12**

March 26

JESUS SAID:

1. Ask and it shall be given you. - **Matthew 7:7**

2. Seek and you shall find. - **Matthew 7:7**

3. Knock, and it shall be open to you. - **Matthew 7:7**

4. Everyone that asketh receiveth. - **Matthew 7:8**

5. He that seeketh findeth. - **Matthew 7:8**

6. To him that knocketh, it shall be opened. - **Matthew 7:8**

7. Whatsoever you desire or you would that men should do to you, do you ever so to them. - **Matthew 7:12**

8. My words that I speak to you are spirit and life. - **John 6:63**

9. Judge not according to the appearance but judge righteous judgement. - **John 7:24**

10. Be not afraid. - **John 6:20**

March 27

JESUS SAID:

1. Be still. - Psalm 46:10, - **Mark 4:39**

2. I am Alpha and Omega, the beginning and the ending. - **Revelation 1:11**

3. I am you hope of glory. - **Matthew 6:13**

4. Heaven and earth shall pass away, but my words shall not pass away! - **Matthew 24:35**

5. All power is given unto me in Heaven and earth. - **Matthew 28:18**

6. I am with you always, even to the end of the world. - **Matthew 28:20**

7. The time is fulfilled, and the kingdom of God is at hand repent ye, and believe the gospel. - **Mark 1:15**

8. I have the power on earth to forgive sin. - **Mark 2:10**

9. Follow me. - **Mark 2:14**

10. But he that shall blaspheme against the Holy Ghost hath never forgiveness, but is in danger of eternal damnation. - **Mark 3:28-29**

March 28

JESUS SAID:

1. Why callest thou me good? There is none good but one, that is God. - **Mark 10:18**

2. If thou can believe, all things are possible to you. - **Mark 9:23**

3. Knoweth the commandments of God. - **Mark 10:19**

4. Do not commit adultery. - **Mark 10:19**

5. Do not kill. - **Mark 10:19**

6. Do not steal. - **Mark 10:19**

7. Do not bear false witness. - **Mark 10:19**

8. Defraud not. - **Mark 10:19**

9. Honor thy father and thy mother. - **Mark 10:19**

10. Follow me. - **Mark 10:21**

March 29
JESUS SAID:

1. The Father himself loveth you because you have loved me and believed that I came out from God. - **John 16:27**

2. I came from the Father and I come into the world. - **John 16:28**

3. I leave the world and go to the Father. - **John 16:28**

4. Do you now believe? - **John 16:31**

5. I am not alone because the Father is with me. - **John 16:32**

6. These things I have spoken to you, that in me ye might have peace might have peace. - **John 16:33**

7. In the world you shall have tribulations but be of good cheer. - John 16:33

8. I have overcome the world. - **John 16:33**

9. I have glorified thee on earth. - **John 17:4**

10. I have finished the work which thou gavest me to do, and now, O' Father, glorify thou me with thine own self with the glory which I had with thee before the world was.
    - **John 17:4-5**

March 30

JESUS SAID:

1. *All power is given to me in Heaven and in earth.*
   - **Matthew 28:18**

2. *I am with you always, even to the end of the world.*
   - **Matthew 28:20**

3. *I will be thou clean.* *-* **Mark 1:41**

4. *Come ye after me.* *-* **Mark 1:17**

5. *Thy sins be forgiven thee.* *-* **Mark 2:5**

6. *Peace be still.* *-* **Mark 4:39**

7. *Be not afraid only believe.* *-* **Mark 6:50**

8. *Be of good cheer.* *-* **Mark 6:50**

9. *Be not afraid.* *-* **Mark 6:50**

10. *Have faith in God.* *-* **Mark 11:22**

March 31

JESUS SAID:

1. *Peace be unto you.* - **John 20:19**

2. *Shew how great things God hath done unto thee.* - **Luke 8:39**

3. *Fear not, believe only.* - **Luke 8:50**

4. *Whom say you that I am?* - **Luke 9:20**

5. *I come not to destroy men's lives but to save them.* - **Luke 9:56**

6. *I give you the power to tread over all the power of the enemy and nothing shall by any means hurt you.* - **Luke 10:19**

7. *Fear not.* - **Luke 12:7**

8. *Blessed are they that hear the word of God and keep it.* - **Luke 11:28**

9. *Ask and it shall be given you.* - **Luke 11:9**

10. *Everyone that asketh receiveth.* - **Luke 11:10**

April 1

JESUS SAID:

1. Your Father knows things you have need of before you ask him. - **Matthew 6:8**

2. Take therefore no thought for the morrow, for the morrow shall take thought for the things of itself. - **Matthew 6:34**

3. Sufficient unto the day is the evil thereof. - **Matthew 6:34**

4. Judge not, that you be not judged. - **Matthew 7:1**

5. For with what judgement ye judge, ye shall be judged. - **Matthew 7:2**

6. I will come and heal him. - **Matthew 8:7**

7. I will, be thou clean. - **Matthew 8:3**

8. Go thy way as thou hast believed, so be it done unto thee. - **Matthew 8:13**

9. Why are you fearful, o ye of little faith? - **Matthew 8:36**

10. Be of good comfort, thy faith has made thee whole. - **Matthew 9:22**

April 2

JESUS SAID:

1. I send the promises of my Father upon you. - **Luke 24:49**

2. Wait, until ye be endued with power from on high. - **Luke 24:49**

3. Why are you troubled? And why do thoughts arise in your heart? - **Luke 24:38**

4. Peace be unto you. - **Luke 24:36**

5. I must be delivered into the hands of sinful men, and be crucified and the third day rise again. - Luke 24:7

6. Father, forgive them for they know not what they do. - **Luke 23:34**

7. Hereafter I, (the Son of man) shall sit on the right hand of the power of God. - **Luke 22:69**

8. Why sleep ye ? Rise and pray, lest ye enter into temptation. - **Luke 22:46**

9. Pray that you not enter into temptation. - **Luke 22:40**

10. What wilt thou that I shall do unto thee? - **Luke 18:41**

April 3

JESUS SAID:

1. *All power is given unto me in Heaven and in earth.*
   - **Matthew 28:18**

2. *I am with you always, even unto the end of the world.*
   - **Matthew 28:20**

3. *Be not afraid.* - **Matthew 28:10**

4. *After three days I will rise again.* - **Matthew 27:63**

5. *That he that believeth and is baptized shall be saved.*
   - **Mark 16:16**

6. *Have faith in God.* - **Mark 11:22**

7. *Whosoever believed in his heart those things which he saith shall come to pass; he shall have whatsoever he saith.*
   - **Mark 11:23**

8. *I came not to be ministered unto but to minister and to give my life a ransom for many.* - **Mark 10:45**

9. *What will you that I should do unto you?* - **Mark 10:51**

10. *Go thy way, thy faith has made thee whole.* - **Mark 10:52**

April 4

JESUS SAID:

1. Neither pray I for these alone, I pray also for them which shall believe on me through their word. - **John 17:20**

2. I pray that thou should keep them from evil. - **John 17:15**

3. They are not of the world even as I am not of the world. - **John 17:16**

4. Sanctify them through thy truth. - **John 17:17**

5. Thy word is truth. - **John 17:17**

6. The glory which thou gavest me I have given them; that they may be one, even as we are one. - **John 17:22**

7. I pray for them. - **John 17:9**

8. Of them which thou gavest me, I have lost none. - **John 18:9**

9. My kingdom is not of this world. - **John 18:36**

10. It is finished. - **John 19:30**

April 5

JESUS SAID:

1. He that believeth upon me, the works that I do shall he do also. - **John 14:12**

2. Greater works than these shall he do because I go to my Father. - **John 14:12**, 14

3. Whatsoever you ask in my name that I will do, that the Father may be glorified in the Son. - **John 14:13**

4. If you love me keep my commandments. - **John 14:14**

5. I will pray the Father and he shall give you another Comforter. - **John 14:16**

6. That he may abide with you forever. - **John 14:16**

7. The Comforter you will know him for He dwelleth with you and shall be in you. - **John 14:17**

8. I will not leave you comfortless. - **John 14:18**

9. He it is that love me, shall be loved by my Father. - **John 14:21**

10. I will also love you and will manifest myself to you. - **John 14:21**

April 6

JESUS SAID:

1. Most assuredly unless one is born of water and the spirit, he cannot enter the kingdom of God. - **John 3:5**

2. I am the true vine. - **John 15:1**

3. My Father is the husbandman. - **John 15:1**

4. Every branch in me that does not bear fruit he takes away. - **John 15:2**

5. Every branch that bears fruit, he prunes, that it may bear more fruit. - **John 15:2**

6. Now you are clean through the word which I have spoken to you. - **John 15:3**

7. Abide in me, and I in you. - **John 15:4**

8. As a branch cannot bear fruit of itself unless it abides in the vine neither can you unless you abide in me. - **John 15:4**

9. I am the vine. - **John 15:3**

10. You are the branches. - **John 15:5**

April 7

JESUS SAID:

1. He who abides in me and I in him bears much fruit. – **John 15:5**

2. Without me you can do nothing. – **John 15:5**

3. If anyone does not abide in me, he is cast out as a branch and is withered; and men gather them and cast them into the fire, and they are burned. – **John 15:6**

4. If you abide in me and my words abide in you, you will ask what you desire, and it shall be done unto you. – **John 15:7**

5. By this my Father is glorified. – **John 15:8**

6. That you bear much fruit. – **John 15:8**

7. You will be my disciples. – **John 15:8**

8. As the Father loved me. – **John 15:9**

9. I also loved you. – **John 15:9**

10. Continue ye in my love. – **John 15:9**

April 8

JESUS SAID:

1. Be of good cheer; It is I . - **Matthew 14:27**

2. Do not be afraid. - **Matthew 14:27**

3. Come to me. - **Matthew 15:29**

4. O you of little faith, why did you doubt. - **Matthew 15:31**

5. Arise, and do not be afraid. - **Matthew 17:7**

6. If you have faith as a mustard seed, you will say to this mountain, move from here to there and nothing will be impossible to you. - **Matthew 17:20**

7. Bring them to me. - **Matthew 14:18**

8. Hear and understand. - **Matthew 15:10**

9. Assuredly, whatever you bind on earth will be bound in Heaven. - **Matthew 18:18**

10. Whatever you loose on earth will be loosed in Heaven. - **Matthew 18:18**

April 9

JESUS SAID:

1. Peace be with you. – **John 20:19**

2. Peace be unto you, as my Father hath sent me, even so, I send you. – **John 20:21**

3. Receive ye the Holy Spirit. – **John 20:22**

4. If you forgive the sins of any, they are forgiven unto them. – **John 20:23**

5. If you retain the sins of any they are retained. – **John 20:23**

6. Peace to you. – **John 20:26**

7. Do not be unbelieving but believing. – **John 20:27**

8. Blessed are those who have not seen and yet have believed. – **John 20:29**

9. Do you love me. ? – **John 21: 15,16,17**

10. Feed my lambs, feed my sheep and follow me. – **John 21:15,16,17,19**

April 10

JESUS SAID:

1. Let not your heart be troubled. - **John 14:1**

2. I am the way, the truth, and the life. - **John 14:6**

3. Most assuredly, I say to you, he who believes in me, the works that I do he will do also. - **John 14:12**

4. And greater works than these he will do. - **John 14:12**

5. Because I go to my Father. - **John 14:12**

6. Whatever you ask in my name, that I will do, that the Father may be glorified in the Son. - **John 14:13**

7. If you ask anything in my name, I will do it. - **John 14:14**

8. If you love me keep my commandments. - **John 14:15**

9. I will pray the Father and he will give you another Comforter, that he may abide with you forever. - **John 14:16**

10. The Spirit of truth; whom the world cannot receive, because it seeth him not, neither knoweth him: but you know him; for he dwelleth with you, and shall be in you. - **John 14:17**

April 11

JESUS SAID:

1. Abide in my love. - **John 15:9**

2. The Comforter, the Holy Spirit, will teach you all things. - **John 14:26**

3. Let not your heart be troubled neither let it be afraid. - **John 14:29**

4. My peace I give to you; peace I leave with you. - **John 14:27**

5. Without me you can do nothing. - **John 15:5**

6. If you abide in me and my words abide in you, you will ask what you desire, and it shall be done for you. - **John 15:7**

7. As the Father loves me, I also have loved you, continue in my love. - **John 15:9**

8. You did not choose me, but I chose you that you should go and bear fruit. - **John 15:16**

9. I chose you that your fruit should remain. - **John 15:16**

10. I command you that you love one another. - **John 15:17**

April 12

JESUS SAID:

1. Come to me all you who labor and are heavy laden and I will give you rest. - **Matthew 11:28**

2. Take my yoke upon you and learn from me, and you will find rest for your souls. - **Matthew 11:29**

3. My yoke is easy and my burden is light. - **Matthew 11:30**

4. He who is not with me is against me. - **Matthew 12:30**

5. For by your words you will be justified, and by your words you will be condemned. - **Matthew 12:37**

6. Whoever does the will of my Father in Heaven is my brother and sister and mother. - **Matthew 12:50**

7. O you of little faith, why did you doubt. - **Matthew 14:31**

8. I am the bread of life. - **John 6:35**

9. I am the bread which came down from Heaven. - **John 6:41**

10. It is written in the prophets and they shall be all taught of God. - **John 6:45**

April 13

JESUS SAID:

1. *If you can believe, all things are possible to him who believe.* - **Mark 9:23**

2. *With God, all things are possible.* - **Mark 10:27**

3. *What do you want me to do for you?* - **Mark 10:51**

4. *Go thy way, thy faith has made thee whole.* - **Mark 10:52**

5. *Have faith in God.* - **Mark 11:22**

6. *Therefore, I say to you, whatever things you ask when you pray, believe that you receive them and you will have them.* - **Mark 11:24**

7. *Whenever you stand praying, if you have anything against anyone forgive him, that your Father in Heaven may also forgive you.* - **Mark 11:26**

8. *Heaven and earth will pass away, but my words will by no means pass away.* - **Mark 13:31**

9. *And what I say to you, I say to all; Watch.* - **Mark 13:37**

10. *Watch therefore, for you do not know when the Master of the house is coming.* – **Mark 13:35**

April 14

JESUS SAID:

1. I am the light of the world. - **John 8:12**

2. He who follows me shall not walk in darkness but have the light of life. - **John 8:12**

3. If anyone thirst let him come to me and drink. - **John 7:37**

4. He who believes on me, as the scripture has said, out of his heart will flow rivers of living water. - **John 7:38**

5. My doctrine is not mine, but his who sent me. - **John 7:16**

6. Do not judge according to appearance, but judge with righteous judgements. - **John 7:24**

7. Do you believe on the Son of God? - **John 9:35**

8. I am the good shepherd. - **John 10:11**

9. I lay down my life for the sheep. - **John 10:15**

10. I know my sheep and am known by my own. - **John 10:14**

April 15

JESUS SAID:

1. And you shall know the truth and the truth shall make you free. - **John 8:32**

2. God is a Spirit and those who worship him must worship in spirit and truth. - **John 4:24**

3. I that speak to you am he. - **John 4:26**

4. I have meat to eat of which you do not know. - **John 4:32**

5. My meat is to do the will of he who sent me and to finish his work. - **John 4:35**

6. I sent you to reap that for which you have not labored; others have labored, and you have entered into their labor. - **John 4:38**

7. Do not judge according to appearance, but judge with righteous judgement. - **John 7:24**

8. He that believeth on me, as the scripture has said out of his heart will flow rivers of living water. - **John 7:38**

9. I am the door. - **John 10:9**

10. I am the resurrection and the life; he that believeth in me, though he were dead, yet shall he live; - **John 11:25**

April 16

JESUS SAID:

1. Ye shall be sorrowful, but your sorrow shall be turned into joy. - **John 16:20**

2. Your heart shall rejoice, and your joy no man taketh from you. - **John 16:22**

3. Whatsoever ye ask the Father in my name, he will give it you. - **John 16:23**

4. The time cometh, when I shall no more speak unto you in proverbs, but I shall shew you plainly of the Father. - **John 16:25**

5. For the Father himself loveth you because you have loved me, and believed that I came out from God. - **John 16:27**

6. These things I have spoken to you that in me ye might have peace. - **John 16:33**

7. In the world ye shall have tribulations. - **John 16:33**

8. Be of good cheer. - **John 16:33**

9. I have overcome the world. - **John 16:33**

10. As the Father has given his Son power over all flesh, that he should give eternal life to as many as God has given him. - **John 17:2**

April 17

JESUS SAID:

1. If ye have faith, and doubt not, ye shall not only do this which is done to the fig tree. - **Matthew 21:21**

2. Also if ye say unto this mountain, be thou removed, and be thou cast into the sea, it shall be done. - **Matthew 21:21**

3. And all things, whatsoever ye shall ask in prayer, believing, ye shall receive. - **Matthew 21:22**

4. Ye do err, not knowing the scripture, nor the power of God. - **Matthew 22:29**

5. Thou shalt love the Lord, thy God with all thy heart and with all thy soul and with all thy mind. - **Matthew 22:37**

6. This is the first and great commandment. - **Matthew 22:38**

7. And the second is like unto it, thou shalt love thy neighbor as thyself. - **Matthew 22:39**

8. On these two commandments hang all the law and the prophets. - **Matthew 22:40**

9. Call no man your father upon the earth for one is your Father, which is in Heaven. - **Matthew 23:9**

10. Neither be ye called master for one is your Master, even Christ. - **Matthew 23:10**

April 18

JESUS SAID:

1. It is written man shall not live by bread alone. - **Matthew 4:4**

2. Man shall live by every word that proceed out of the mouth of God. - **Matthew 4:4**

3. It is written again, thou shall not tempt the Lord thy God. - **Matthew 4:7**

4. Get thee hence, Satan: for it is written, Thou shalt worship the Lord thy God, and him only shalt thou serve. - **Matthew 4:10**

5. Follow me. - **Matthew 4:19**

6. Ask and it shall be given you. - **Matthew 7:7**

7. Seek and you shall find. - **Matthew 7:7**

8. Knock, and it shall be opened to you. - **Matthew 7:7**

9. For everyone who ask receiveth; and he that seeketh findeth, and to him that knocketh, it shall be opened. - **Matthew 7:8**

10. If ye then being evil, know how to give good gifts unto your children how much more shall your Father which is in Heaven give good gifts to them who ask him? - **Matthew 7:11**

April 19

JESUS SAID:

1. It is written, That man shall not live by bread alone, but by every word of God. - **Luke 4:4**

2. Thou shalt worship the Lord thy God, and him only shalt thou serve. - **Luke 4:8**

3. Thou shall not tempt the Lord thy God. - **Luke 4:12**

4. The Spirit of the Lord is upon me. - **Luke 4:18**

5. The Spirit of the Lord has anointed me to preach the gospel to the poor. - **Luke 4:18**

6. He has sent me to heal the broken hearted. - **Luke 4:18**

7. He has sent me to preach deliverance to the captives. - **Luke 4:18**

8. He has sent me to recover the sight of the blind. - **Luke 4:18**

9. The Spirit of the Lord has sent me to set at liberty them that are bruised. - **Luke 4:18**

10. This day is this scripture fulfilled in your ears. - **Luke 4:21**

April 20

JESUS SAID:

1. Peace be still. - **Mark 4:39**

2. The time is fulfilled. - **Mark 1:15**

3. The kingdom of God is at hand. - **Mark 1:15**

4. Repent ye. **Mark 1:15**

5. Believe the gospel. - **Mark 1:15**

6. Come ye after me. - **Mark 1:17**

7. I will, be thou clean. - **Mark 1:41**

8. Son thy sins be forgiven thee. - **Mark 2:5**

9. That ye may know that the Son of man hath power on earth to forgive sins. - **Mark 2:10**

10. I came not to call the righteous, but sinners to repentance. - **Mark 2:17**

April 21

JESUS SAID:

1. What wilt thou that I shall do unto thee. - **Luke 18:41**

2. The things which is impossible with men are possible with God. - **Luke 18:27**

3. Verily I say unto you, whosoever shall not receive the kingdom of God as a little child shall in no wise enter therein. - **Luke 18:17**

4. For the Son of man is come to seek and to save that which was lost. - **Luke 19:10**

5. Pray that ye enter not into temptation. - **Luke 22:40**

6. Take no thought of your life, what ye shall eat, neither for the body, what ye shall put on. - **Luke 12:22**

7. Life is more than meat, and the body more than raiment. - **Luke 12:23**

8. Consider the ravens and God feedeth them, how much more are you better than the fouls. - **Luke 12:24**

9. Which of you with taking thought can add to your stature one cubit. - **Luke 12:25**

10. Your Father knows you have need of these things, eating, drinking and clothings, etc. - **Luke 12:30**

April 22

JESUS SAID:

1. That ye shall die in your sins, for if ye believe not that I am he, ye shall die in your sins. - **John 8:24**

2. I am from above: ye are of this world; I am not of this world. - **John 8:23**

3. He that sent me is true, and I speak to the world those things which I have heard of him. - **John 8:26**

4. I do nothing of myself, but as my Father hath taught me, I speak these things. - **John 8:28**

5. And he that sent me is with me: the Father has not left me alone. - **John 8:29**

6. I do always those things that please Him. - **John 8:29**

7. If ye continue in my word, then you are my disciples indeed. - **John 8:31**

8. You shall know the truth and the truth shall make you free. - **John 8:32**

9. Verily, verily, I say unto you, Whosoever committeth sin is the servant of sin. - **John 8:34**

10. If the Son shall make you free you are free indeed. - **John 8:36**

April 23

JESUS SAID:

1. Take heed, and beware of covetousness. - **Luke 12:15**
2. Man's life consists not in the abundance of the things which he possesseth. - **Luke 12:15**
3. For where your treasure is, there will your heart be also. - **Luke 12:34**
4. Blessed are those servants; whom the Lord when he cometh shall find watching. - **Luke 12:37**
5. Blessed is that servant; whom his Lord when he cometh shall find so doing. - **Luke 12:43**
6. Of truth I say unto you, he will make him ruler over all he hath. - **Luke 12:44**
7. Except ye repent, ye shall all likewise perish. - **Luke 13:3**
8. Unto what is the kingdom of God like? and whereunto shall I resemble it? - **Luke 13:18**
9. It is like a grain of mustard seed. - **Luke 13:19**
10. It grew and waxed a great tree. - **Luke 13:19**

April 24

JESUS SAID:

1. It is written that man shall not live by bread alone, but by every word of God. - **Luke 4:4**

2. For it is written thou shalt worship the Lord thy God, and him only shalt thou serve. - **Luke 4:8**

3. Thou shall not tempt the Lord thy God. - **Luke 4:12**

4. The Spirit of the Lord is upon me. - **Luke 4:18**

5. He hath sent me to preach the gospel to the poor. - **Luke 4:18**

6. He has sent me to heal the broken hearted. - **Luke 4:18**

7. He has sent me to preach deliverance to the captive.
   - **Luke 4:18**

8. He has sent me to recover sight to the blind. - **Luke 4:18**

9. He has sent me to set at liberty them that are bruised.
   - **Luke 4:18**

10. He has sent me to preach the acceptable year of the Lord.
    - **Luke 4:19**

April 25

JESUS SAID:

1. He that sent me is with me. - **John 8:29**

2. The Father hath not left me alone. - **John 8:29**

3. I do always those things that please him. - **John 8:29**

4. If you continue in my word, then you are my disciples indeed. - **John 8:31**

5. Ye shall know the truth and the truth shall make you free. - **John 8:32**

6. The Son abideth forever. - **John 8:35**

7. If the Son therefore shall make you free, ye shall be free indeed. - **John 8:36**

8. I speak that which I have seen with my Father. - **John 8:38**

9. You do that what you have seen with your father. - **John 8:38**

10. If God were your Father, ye would love me for I proceed forth and came from God; neither came I of myself, but he sent me. - **John 8:42**

April 26

JESUS SAID:

1. Fear not; from henceforth thou shalt catch men. - **Luke 5:10**

2. I will ; be thou clean. - **Luke 5:13**

3. Man, thy sins are forgiven thee. - **Luke 5:20**

4. What reason ye in your hearts? - **Luke 5:22**

5. Follow me. - **Luke 5:27**

6. I came not to call the righteous, but sinners to repentance. - **Luke 5:32**

7. No man putteth a piece of new garment upon an old. - **Luke 5:36**

8. The piece that was taken out of the new agreeth not with the old. - **Luke 5:36**

9. No man putteth new wine into old bottles. - **Luke 5:37**

10. The new wine will burst the bottles and the bottles shall perish, new wine must be put into new bottles and both are preserved. - **Luke 5:37-38**

April 27

JESUS SAID:

1. Verily, verily I say unto you, Except ye be converted and become as little children, ye shall not enter into the kingdom of Heaven. - **Matthew 18:3**
2. Whosoever therefore shall humble himself as a little child, the same is greatest in the kingdom of Heaven. - **Matthew 18:4**
3. Who shall receive one such little child in my name receive me. - **Matthew 18:5**
4. Whoso shall offend one of these little ones which believe in me, it were better for him that a millstone were hanged about his neck and he were drowned in depth of the sea. – **Matthew 18:6**
5. Take heed that ye despise not one of these little ones, I say unto you that in Heaven their angels do always behold the face of my Father which is in Heaven. - **Matthew 18:10**
6. The Son of man is come to save that which was lost. – **Matthew 18:11**
7. It is not the will of your Father which is in Heaven that one of these little ones shall perish. - **Matthew 18:14**
8. Suffer little children and forbid them not to come unto me. – **Matthew 19:14**
9. For such is the kingdom of Heaven. - **Matthew 19:14**
10. If thou wilt enter into life, keep the commandments – **Matthew 19:17**

April 28

JESUS SAID:

1. *I am the light of the world.* - **John 8:12**

2. *He that follows me shall not walk in darkness.* - **John 8:12**

3. *They that follow me shall have the light of life.* - **John 8:12**

4. *I bear record of myself.* - **John 8:14**

5. *My record is true, for I know whence I came, and whither I go.* - **John 8:14**

6. *Ye cannot tell whence I come, and whither I go.* - **John 8:14**

7. *Ye judge after the flesh.* - **John 8:15**

8. *I judge no man.* - **John 8:15**

9. *Ye shall die in your sins, if ye believe not that I am he, ye shall die in your sins.* - **John 8:24**

10. *He that sent me is true, and I speak to the world those things which I have heard of him.* - **John 8:26**

April 29

JESUS SAID:

1. It is expedient for you that I go away. - **John 16:7**

2. For if I go not away, the Comforter will not come unto you. - **John 16:7**

3. If I depart, I will send him unto you. - **John 16:7**

4. When he comes, he will reprove the world of sin, and of righteousness and of judgment. - **John 16:8**

5. Of sin, because they believe not on me. - **John 16:9**

6. Of righteousness, because I go to my Father, and you see me no more. - **John 16:10**

7. Of judgment because the prince of the world is judged. - **John 16:11**

8. When the Spirit of truth comes, he will guide you into all truths. - **John 16:13**

9. He shall not speak of himself, but whatsoever he shall hear, that shall he speak. - **John 16:13**

10. He will shew you things to come. - **John 16:13**

April 30

JESUS SAID:

1. *My grace is sufficient for thee.* - **II Corinthians 12:9**

2. *For my strength is made perfect in weakness.*
   - **II Corinthians 12:9**

3. *Peace I leave with you., my peace I give unto you . Let not your heart be troubled, neither let it be afraid.*
   - **John 14:27**

4. *I go unto the Father.* - **John 14:28**

5. *For my Father is greater than I.* - **John 14:28**

6. *Abide in me and I in you.* - **John 15:4**

7. *Without me, ye can do nothing.* - **John 15:5**

8. *If ye abide in me, and my words abide in you, ye shall ask what ye will, and it shall be done unto you.* - **John 15:7**

10. *Herein is my Father glorified, that you bear much fruit.*
    - **John 15:8**

May 1

JESUS SAID:

1. My mother and brethren are those which hear the word of God and do it. - **Luke 8:21**

2. Where is your faith- **Luke 8:25**

3. Return to thine own house and shew how great things God hath done unto thee. - **Luke 8:39**

4. Be of good comfort : thy faith hath made thee whole, go in peace. - **Luke 8:48**

5. Fear not, believe only and be made whole. - **Luke 8:50**

6. Whom say ye, that I am. - **Luke 9:20**

7. If any man will come after me, let him deny himself, and take up his cross daily, and follow me. - **Luke 9:23**

8. Whosoever will save his life shall lose it. - **Luke 9:24**

9. Whosoever will lose his life for my sake, the same shall save it. - **Luke 9:24**

10. For what is a man advantage, if he gains the whole world, and lose himself, or he is cast away? - **Luke 9:25**

May 2

JESUS SAID:

1. I am come that you might have life, and that you might have it more abundantly. - **John 10:10**

2. I am the good shepherd. - **John 10:11**

3. The good shepherd giveth his life for the sheep. - **John 10:11**

4. I know my sheep and am known of mine. - **John 10:14**

5. As the Father knoweth me, even so know I the Father: and I lay down my life for the sheep. - **John 10:15**

6. Other sheep, I have which are not of this fold. - **John 10:16**

7. Them also I must bring and they shall hear my voice. - **John 10:16**

8. There shall be one fold, and one shepherd. - **John 10:16**

9. I have the power to lay my life down and take it up again. - **John 10:18**

10. This commandment have I received of my Father. - **John 10:18**

May 3

JESUS SAID:

1. Let not your heart be troubled. - **John 14:1**
2. Ye believe in God believe in me also. - **John 14:1**
3. In my Father's house are many mansions.- **John 14:2**
4. I go to prepare a place for you. - **John 14:3**
5. I will come again. - **John 14:3**
6. I will receive you to myself. - **John 14:3**
7. That where I am, ye may be also. - **John 14:3**
8. Whither I go ye know, and the way ye know. - **John 14:4**
9. I am the way the truth and the life. - **John 14:6**
10. No man cometh unto the Father but by me. - **John 14:6**

May 4

JESUS SAID:

1. I have meat to eat that ye know not. - **John 4:32**
2. My meat is to do the will of him that sent me and to finish his work. - **John 4:34**
3. Lift up your eyes, and look on the fields, for they are white already to harvest. - **John 4:35**
4. He that reapeth receives wages. - **John 4:36**
5. And he gathereth fruit unto life eternal. - **John 4:36**
6. That he that both soweth and he that reapeth may rejoice together. - **John 4:36**
7. Herein is that saying true, one soweth and another reapeth. - **John 4:37**
8. I sent you to reap that whereon ye bestowed no labor. - **John 4:38**
9. Other men labored and ye are entered into their labours. - **John 4:38**
10. Except you see signs and wonders, ye will not believe. - **John 4:48**

May 5

JESUS SAID:

1. It is written that man shall not live by bread alone, but by every word of God. - **Luke 4:4**

2. Get thee behind me Satan. - **Luke 4:8**

3. For it is written thou shalt worship the Lord thy God and him only shalt thou serve. - **Luke 4:8**

4. Thou shall not tempt the Lord thy God. - **Luke 4:12**

5. The Spirit of the Lord is upon me. - **Luke 4:18**

6. He has anointed me to preach the gospel to the poor. - **Luke 4:18**

7. He has sent me to heal the broken-hearted. - **Luke 4:18**

8. He has sent me to preach deliverance to the captives. - **Luke 4:18**

9. He has sent me to recover sight to the blind. - **Luke 4:18**

10. He has sent me to set at liberty them that are bruised. - **Luke 4:18**

May 6

JESUS SAID:

1. If ye love me, keep my commandments. - **John 14:15**
2. I will pray the Father, and he shall give you another Comforter, that he may abide with you forever. - **John 14:16**
3. Even the Spirit of truth; whom the world cannot receive. - **John 14:17**
4. The world seeth the Spirit not, neither knoweth him. - **John 14:17**
5. But ye know him; for he dwelleth with you, and shall be in you. - **John 14:17**
6. I will not leave you comfortless, I will come to you. - **John 14:18**
7. Yet a little while, and the world see me no more. - **John 14:19**
8. But ye see me; because I live, ye shall live also. - **John 14:19**
9. At that day ye shall know that I am in my Father, and ye in me, and I in you. - **John 14:20**
10. He that hath my commandments and keepeth them, loveth me and shall be loved of my Father and I will love him and will manifest myself to him. - **John 14:21**

May 7

JESUS SAID:

1. I am the light of the world. - **John 8:12**

2. He that followeth me shall not walk in darkness, but shall have the light of life. - **John 8:12**

3. My record is true, for I know whence I came, and whither I go; but ye cannot tell whither I come or whither I go. - **John 8:14**

4. Ye judge after the flesh, I judge no man. - **John 8:15**

5. Yet, if f I judge, my judgement is true, for I am not alone, but I and the Father that sent me. - **John 8:16**

6. If you believe not that I am he, ye shall die in your sins. - **John 8:24**

7. I do nothing of myself; but as my Father hath taught me, I speak these things. - **John 8:28**

8. He that sent me is with me. - **John 8:29**

9. The Father has not left me alone. - **John 8:29**

10. For I do always those things that please him. - **John 8:29**

May 8

JESUS SAID:

1. It is finished. - **John 19:30**

2. Peace be unto you. - **John 20:19**

3. Peace be unto you, as my Father hath sent me, even so I send you. - **John 20:21**

4. Receive ye the Holy Ghost. - **John 20:22**

5. Be not faithless but believing. - **John 20:27**

6. Blessed are they that have not seen, and yet have believed. - **John 20:29**

7. Loveth thou me? Feed my sheep. - **John 21:16**

8. Follow me. - **John 21:19**

9. Follow thou me. - **John 21:22**

10. If I will, that he tarry till I come, what is that to thee? follow thou me. - **John 21:22**

May 9

JESUS SAID:

1. *I am with you always, even to the end of the world.*
   - **Matthew 28:20**

2. *He that has ears to hear, let him hear.* - **Mark 4:9, 23**

3. *Unto you that hear shall more be given.* - **Mark 4:24**

4. *The kingdom of God is like a grain of mustard seed.*
   - **Mark 4:31**

5. *When it is sown in the earth, it grows up and becomes greater than all the herbs.* - **Mark 4:32**

6. *Unto you it is given to know the mystery of the kingdom of God.* - **Mark 4:11**

7. *The sower soweth the word.* - **Mark 4:14**

8. *Hear the word, receive it and allow the word to bring forth fruit, some thirtyfold, some sixty, and some an hundred.*
   - **Mark 4:20**

9. *For there is nothing hid, which shall not be manifested.*
   - **Mark 4:22**

10. *Neither was anything kept secret, but that it should come abroad.* - **Mark 4:22**

May 10

JESUS SAID:

1. I am the true vine, my Father is the husbandman. - **John 15:1**
2. You are the branches for without me you can do nothing. - **John 15:5**
3. He that abideth in me, and I in him, the same bringeth forth much fruit. - **John 15:5**
4. Every branch in me that beareth not fruit he taketh away; and every branch that beareth fruit, the Father purgeth it, that it may bring forth more fruit. - **John 15:2**
5. If a man abide not in me, he withers and men gather them and cast them into the fire, and they are burned. - **John 15:6**
6. If ye abide in me and my words abide in you, ye shall ask what you will - **John 15:7**
7. And it shall be done unto you. - **John 15:7**
8. Herein is my Father glorified, that you bear much fruit, so shall you be my disciples- **John 15:8**
9. As the Father has loved me, so have I loved you: continue ye in my love. - **John 15:9**
10. If you keep my commandments you shall abide in my love. - **John 15:10**

May 11

JESUS SAID:

1. Let not your heart be troubled. - **John 14:1**
2. Ye believe in God believe also in me. - **John 14:1**
3. In my Father's house are many mansions ; I go to prepare a place for you. - **John 14:2**
4. I will come again. - **John 14:3**
5. And receive you unto myself. - **John 14:3**
6. That where I am, there ye may be also. - **John 14:3**
7. Where I go you know, and the way you know. - **John 14:4**
8. I am the way. - **John 14:6**
9. I am the life. - **John 14:6**
10. I am the truth, no man cometh unto the Father but by me. - **John 14:6**

May 12

JESUS SAID:

1. Come unto me all ye that labor and are heavy laden, and I will give you rest. - **Matthew 11:28**

2. Take my yoke upon you and learn of me. - **Matthew 11:29**

3. I am meek and lowly in heart. - **Matthew 11:29**

4. Ye shall find rest unto your soul. - **Matthew 11:29**

5. My yoke is easy and my burden light. - **Matthew 11:30**

6. These things have I spoken to you that my joy might remain in you, and that your joy might be full. - **John 15:11**

7. This is my commandment that you love one another, as I have loved you. - **John 15:12**

8. I have called you friends; for all things that I have heard of my Father I have made known to you. - **John 15:15**

9. Ye are my friends if you do whatever I command you. - **John 15:14**

10. Greater love has no man than this, that he lay down his life for his friends. - **John 15:13**

May 13

JESUS SAID:

1. Who say you that I am? - **Mark 8:29**

2. Whosoever will come after me let him deny himself, and take up his cross and follow me. - **Mark 8:34**

3. Whosoever save his life, shall lose it. - **Mark 8:35**

4. Whosoever shall lose his life for my sake and the gospel's, the same shall save it. - **Mark 8:35**

5. What shall it profit a man, if he gain the whole world, and lose his soul? - **Mark 8:36**

6. Or what shall a man give in exchange for his soul. - **Mark 8:37**

7. Whosoever therefore shall be ashamed of me and of my words in this adulterous and sinful generation; of him shall the Son of man be ashamed. - **Mark 8:38**

8. When he cometh in the glory of his Father with the holy angels. - **Mark 8:38**

9. Get thee behind me Satan. - **Mark 8:33**

10. For thou savourest not the things that be of God but the things that be of men. - **Mark 8:33**

May 14

JESUS SAID:

1. With God all things are possible. - **Mark 10:27**
2. With men it is impossible, but not with God. - **Mark 10:27**
3. The Son of man came to minister and to give his life a ransom for many. - **Mark 10:45**
4. What wilt thou that I should do unto thee? - **Mark 10:51**
5. Go thy way; thy faith hath made thee whole. - **Mark 10:52**
6. Have faith in God. - **Mark 11:22**
7. Verily I say unto you, whosoever shall say unto this mountain, be thou removed and be cast into the sea, and shall not doubt in his heart, but shall believe that those things which he saith shall come to pass, he shall have whatsoever he saith. - **Mark 11:23**
8. What things soever you desire, when ye pray, believe that you receive them, and you shall have them
   - **Mark 11:24; John 15:7;** - **John 16:24**
9. When you stand praying, forgive. - **Mark 11:25**
10. If you have aught against any, that your Father also which is in Heaven may forgive you your trespasses. - **Mark 11:25**

May 15

JESUS SAID:

1. Have faith in God. - **Mark 11:22**

2. When you stand praying, forgive, if ye have ought against any. - **Mark 11:25**

3. And, what I say unto you I say unto all, Watch. - **Mark 13:37**

4. Take ye heed, watch and pray. - **Mark 13:33**

5. Heaven and earth shall pass away; but my words shall not pass away. - **Mark 13:31**

6. Many shall come in my name, saying, I am Christ; and shall deceive many. - **Mark 13:6**

7. Nations shall rise against nations. - **Mark 13:8**

8. The end shall not be yet. - **Mark 13:7**

9. And kingdoms against kingdoms. - **Mark 13:8**

10. There shall be earthquakes in divers places, and there shall be famine and troubles; these are the beginnings of sorrow. - **Mark 13:8**

May 16

JESUS SAID:

1. I thank thee Father, Lord of Heaven and earth. - **Luke 10:21**

2. He that heareth you heareth me. - **Luke 10:16**

3. He that despiseth you despiseth me. - **Luke 10:16**

4. He that despiseth me despiseth him that sent me. - **Luke 10:16**

5. I beheld Satan as lightning fall from Heaven. - **Luke 10:18**

6. Behold I give you power to tread on serpents and scorpions, and over all the power of the enemy and nothing shall by any means hurt you. - **Luke 10:19**

7. Rejoice not in this, that the spirits are subject to you, but rather rejoice because your names are written in Heaven. - **Luke 10:20**

8. Thou hast hid these things from the wise and prudent. - **Luke 10:21**

9. He has revealed them unto babes. - **Luke 10:21**

10. For so it seemed good in thy sight. - **Luke 10:21**

May 17

JESUS SAID:

1. Hear and understand. - **Matthew 15:10**

2. Not that which goeth into the mouth defileth a man but that which cometh out of the mouth which defileth a man. - **Matthew 15:11**

3. Why do you transgress the commandment of God by your traditions. - **Matthew 15:3**

4. Do not ye yet understand that whatsoever entereth the mouth goeth into the belly, and is cast out into the draught. - **Matthew 15:17**

5. Those things which proceed out of the mouth comes forth from the heart, and they defile the man. - **Matthew 15:18**

6. For out of the heart proceed evil thoughts, murders, adulteries, fornications, thefts, false witness, blasphemies. - **Matthew 15:19**

7. These are the things which defileth a man. - **Matthew 15:20**

8. But to eat with unwashed hands defileth not a man. - **Matthew 15:20**

9. If any man will come after me, let him deny himself and take up his cross and follow me. - **Matthew 16:24**

10. Whosoever will save his life shall lose it and whosoever will lose his life for my sake shall find it. - **Matthew 16:25**

May 18

JESUS SAID:

1. Except a man be born of water and of the Spirit he cannot enter into the kingdom of God. - **John 3:5**
2. That which is born of the flesh is flesh; and that which is born of Spirit is spirit. - **John 3:6**
3. The wind bloweth and thou hearest the sound, but cannot tell where it comes and where it goes, so is everyone that is born of the Spirit. - **John 3:8**
4. I speak what I do know and testify what I have seen and you do not receive my witness. - **John 3:11**
5. If I have told you earthly things and you believe not how shall you believe Heavenly things? - **John 3:12**
6. No man hath ascended up to Heaven but, he that come down from Heaven. - **John 3:13**
7. Even the Son of man which is in Heaven. - **John 3:13**
8. As Moses lifted up the serpent in the wilderness, even so must the Son of man be lifted up. - **John 3:14**
9. Whosoever believeth in him shall not perish, but have eternal life - **John 3:15**
10. For God so loved the world that he gave his one begotten Son, that whosoever believeth in him shall not perish but have everlasting life. - **John 3:16**

May 19

JESUS SAID:

1. God sent not His Son into the world to condemn the world. – **John 3:17**

2. God sent His Son that the world through Him might be saved. – **John 3:17**

3. He that believeth on Him is not condemned. – **John 3:18**

4. But he that believeth not is condemned already. – **John 3:18**

5. He is condemned because he hath not believed in the name of the only begotten Son of God. – **John 3:18**

6. This is the condemnation that light is come into the world. – **John 3:19**

7. Men loved darkness rather than light, because their deeds were evil. – **John 3:19**

8. Everyone that doeth evil hateth light. – **John 3:20**

9. Neither do they cometh to the light, lest his deeds should be reproved. – **John 3:20**

10. He that doeth truth cometh to the light that his deeds may be manifest, that they are wrought in God. – **John 3:21**

May 20

JESUS SAID:

1. *Let not your heart be troubled.* - **John 14:1**

2. *Ye believe in God, believe in me also.* - **John 14:1**

3. *In my Father's house there are many mansions.* - **John 14:2**

4. *If it was not so I would have told you.* - **John 14:2**

5. *I go to prepare a place for you.* - **John 14:2**

6. *If I go to prepare a place for you I will come again, I will return and receive you unto myself.* - **John 14:3**

7. *That where I am there ye may be also.* - **John 14:3**

8. *Whether I go ye know.* - **John 14:4**

9. *The way you know.* - **John 14:4**

10. *I am the way, the truth and the life, no man cometh unto the Father, but by me.* - **John 14:6**

May 21

JESUS SAID:

1. Whosoever drinketh of the water that I shall give him shall never thirst. - **John 4:13**-14

2. The water that I shall give him shall be in him a well of water springing up into everlasting life. - **John 4:14**

3. The hour cometh, and now is, when the true worshippers shall worship the Father in spirit and in truth. - **John 4:23**

4. The Father seeketh such to worship Him. - **John 4:23**

5. God is a Spirit. - **John 4:24**

6. They that worship Him must worship Him in spirit and in truth. - **John 4:24**

7. My meat is to do the will of Him that sent Me and to finish His work. - **John 4:34**

8. Wilt thou be made whole? - **John 5:6**

9. My Father work hitherto, and I work. - **John 5:17**

10. Verily, verily, I say unto you, the Son can do nothing of himself, but what he seeth the Father do. - **John 5:19**

May 22

JESUS SAID:

1. *If thy brother shall trespass against thee, go and tell him his fault.* - **Matthew 18:15**

2. *Do this between thee and him alone.* - **Matthew 18:15**

3. *If he shall hear thee, thou hast gained thy brother.* - **Matthew 18:15**

4. *If he will not hear thee, take with thee one or two more, that in the mouth of two or three witnesses every word may be established.* - **Matthew 18:16**

5. *If he neglect to hear them tell it to the church.* - **Matthew 18:17**

6. *If he shall neglect to hear the church let him be unto thee as a heathen man and a publican.* - **Matthew 18:17**

7. *Verily, I say unto you, whatsoever, ye shall bind on earth shall be bound in Heaven.* - **Matthew 18:18**

8. *Whatsoever ye shall loose on earth shall be loosed in Heaven.* - **Matthew 18:18**

9. *If two of you shall agree on earth as touching anything that they ask, it shall be done of them of my Father which is in Heaven.* - **Matthew 18:19**

10. *Where two or three are gathered in my name, there I am in the midst of them.* - **Matthew 18:20**

May 23

JESUS SAID:

1. Did I not tell you, If thou wouldest believe, thou shouldest see the glory of God. - **John 11:40**

2. Father I thank Thee that thou hast heard Me. - **John 11:41**

3. Father, I knew that thou hearest Me always. - **John 11:42**

4. To death, loose him and let him go, Lazarus to come forth. - **John 11:43-44**

5. Now is the judgement of the world. - **John 12:31**

6. Now shall the prince of the world be cast out. - **John 12:31**

7. The Son of man must be lifted up. - **John 12:34**

8. I am the way, the truth and the life, no man cometh unto the Father but by Me. - **John 14:6**

9. These things I have spoken to you, that in me ye might have peace, In this world ye shall have tribulations. - **John 16:33**

10. But be of good cheer, I have overcome the world. - **John 16:33**

May 24

JESUS SAID:

1. They that are whole have no need of the physician, but they that are sick. - **Mark 2:17**

2. I came not to call the righteous, but sinners to repentance. - **Mark 2:17**

3. The Sabbath was made for man, and not man for the Sabbath. - **Mark 2:27**

4. The Son of man is Lord also of the Sabbath. - **Mark 2:28**

5. Is it lawful to do good on the Sabbath days or to do evil? To save life or to kill? - **Mark 3:4**

6. How can Satan cast out Satan? - **Mark 3:23**

7. If a kingdom be divided against itself, that kingdom cannot stand. - **Mark 3:24**

8. If a house be divided against itself, that house cannot stand. - **Mark 3:25**

9. If Satan rise up against himself, and be divided, he cannot stand, but hath an end. - **Mark 3:26**

10. No man can enter into a strong man's house and spoil his goods except he will first bind the strong man; and then he will spoil his house. - **Mark 3:27**

May 25

JESUS SAID:

1. I will pray the Father and he shall give you another Comforter that he may abide with you forever. - **John 14:16**

2. Even the Spirit of truth, whom the world cannot receive. - **John 14:17**

3. Whom the world cannot receive because he seeth him not. - **John 14:17**

4. Neither knoweth him, but you know him. - **John 14:17**

5. But you know him for He dwelleth with you and shall be in you. - **John 14:17**

6. I will not leave you comfortless. - **John 14:18**

7. I will come to you. - **John 14:18**

8. Yet a little while, and the world seeth Me no more. - **John 14:19**

9. But ye see Me; because I live, ye shall live also. - **John 14:19**

10. At that day ye shall know that I am in my Father, and Ye in Me and I in you. - **John 14:20**

May 26

JESUS SAID:

1. Ye have not chosen me but I have chosen you. - **John 15:16**

2. I ordained you, that you should go and bring forth fruit. - **John 15:16**

3. And that fruit should remain. - **John 15:16**

4. That whatsoever ye ask of the Father in my name, he may give it you. - **John 15:16**

5. These things I command you that ye love one another. - **John 15:17**

6. If the world hate you, you know that it hated Me before it hated you. - **John 15:18**

7. If ye were of the world the world would love his own. - **John 15:19**

8. But because ye are not of the world but I have chosen you out of the world, therefore the world hateth you. - **John 15:19**

9. Remember the word that I said unto you. - **John 15:20**

10. The servant is not greater than his Lord. - **John 15:20**

May 27

JESUS SAID:

1. Verily I say unto you, all sins shall be forgiven unto the sons of men, and blasphemies wherewith soever they shall blaspheme. - **Mark 3:28**

2. But he that shall blaspheme against the Holy Ghost hath never forgiveness, but is in danger of eternal damnation. - **Mark 3:29**

3. Whosoever shall do the will of God, the same is my brother and my sister, and mother. - **Mark 3:35**

4. There is nothing hid which shall not be manifested. - **Mark 4:22**

5. Neither was anything kept secret but that it should come abroad. - **Mark 4:22**

6. If any man have ears to hear let him hear. - **Mark 4:23**

7. Take heed what ye hear. - **Mark 4:24**

8. With what measure ye mete, it shall be measured to you. - **Mark 4:24**

9. Unto you that hear, shall more be given. - **Mark 4:24**

10. For he that hath, to him shall be given, and he that hath not, from him shall be taken even that which he hath. - **Mark 4:25**

May 28

JESUS SAID:

1. The thief cometh not but to steal and to kill and to destroy. – **John 10:10**

2. I am come that they might have life, and that they might have it more abundantly. – **John 10:10**

3. I am the good shepherd. – **John 10:11**

4. The good shepherd giveth his life for the sheep. – **John 10:11**

5. He that is a hireling, and not the shepherd, whose own the sheep are not, seeth the wolf coming and leaveth the sheep and fleeth. – **John 10:12**

6. And the wolf catcheth them, and scattereth the sheep. – **John 10:12**

7. The hireling fleeth because he is a hireling and careth not for sheep. – **John 10:13**

8. I am the good shepherd and I know my sheep. – **John 10:14**

9. And I am known of mine. – **John 10:14**

10. As the Father knoweth me, even so know I the Father; and I lay down my life for the sheep. – **John 10:15**

May 29

JESUS SAID:

1. Whosoever is angry with his brother without cause shall be in danger of the judgement. - **Matthew 5:22**

2. Whosoever shall say to his brother raca (worthless) shall be in danger of the council: but whosoever shall say thou fool, shall be in danger of hell fire. - **Matthew 5:22**

3. If thou bring thy gift to the altar, and there rememberest that thy brother has ought against thee, leave thy gifts before the altar, and go thy way ; first be reconciled to thy brother. - **Matthew 5:23-24**

4. Then come and offer thy gifts. - **Matthew 5:24**

5. Agree with thine adversary quickly. - **Matthew 5:25**

6. While thou are in the way with him. - **Matthew 5:25**

7. Lest at any time the adversary deliver thee to the judge. - **Matthew 5:25**

8. And the judge deliver thee to the officer, and thou be cast into prison. - **Matthew 5:25**

9. Thou shall by no means come out thence, until thou hast paid the utmost farthing. - **Matthew 5:26**

10. Whosoever shall compel thee to go a mile, go with him two. - **Matthew 5:41**

May 30

JESUS SAID:

1. Give to them that asketh thee. - **Matthew 5:42**

2. From him that would borrow of thee, turn not away.
   - **Matthew 5:42**

3. Love your enemies. - **Matthew 5:44**

4. Bless them that curse you. - **Matthew 5:44**

5. Do good to them that hate you. - **Matthew 5:44**

6. Pray for them that despitefully use you and persecute you.
   - **Matthew 5:44**

7. Do these things that you may be the children of your Father which is in Heaven. - **Matthew 5:45**

8. For your Father maketh his sun to rise on the evil and on the good. - **Matthew 5:45**

9. And your Father sendeth rain on the just and the unjust.
   - **Matthew 5:45**

10. For if ye love them which love you, what reward have you?
    - **Matthew 5:46**

May 31

JESUS SAID:

1. Blessed are the poor in spirit, for theirs is the kingdom of Heaven. - **Matthew 5:3**

2. Blessed are they that mourn, for they shall be comforted. - **Matthew 5:4**

3. Blessed are the meek for they shall inherit the earth. - **Matthew 5:5**

4. Blessed are they which hunger and thirst after righteousness for they shall be filled. - **Matthew 5:6**

5. Blessed are the merciful for they shall obtain mercy. - **Matthew 5:7**

6. Blessed are the pure in heart, for they shall see God. - **Matthew 5:8**

7. Blessed are the peacemakers for they shall be called the children of God. - **Matthew 5:9**

8. Blessed are they which are persecuted for righteousness sake for theirs is the kingdom of Heaven. - **Matthew 5:10**

9. Blessed are ye, when men shall revile you, and persecute you and shall say all manner of evil against you falsely, for my sake. - **Matthew 5:11**

10. Rejoice, and be exceeding glad, for great is your reward in Heaven. - **Matthew 5:12**

June 1

JESUS SAID:

1. *If ye continue in my word, then are ye my disciples indeed.* **– John 8:31**

2. *And ye shall know the truth, and the truth shall make you free.* **– John 8:32**

3. *Ye shall be made free.* **– John 8:33**

4. *Verily, verily, I say unto you, whosoever committeth sin is the servant of sin.* **– John 8:34**

5. *And the servant abideth not in the house forever.* **– John 8:35**

6. *But the Son abideth ever.* **– John 8:35**

7. *If the Son therefore shall make you free, ye shall be free indeed.* **– John 8:36**

8. *I know that ye are Abraham's seed, but you seek to kill me, because my word hath no place in you.* **– John 8:37**

9. *I speak that which I have seen with my Father and you do that which ye have seen with your father.* **– John 8:38**

10. *If ye were Abraham's children, ye would do the works of Abraham.* **– John 8:39**

June 2

JESUS SAID:

1. Take heed that ye do not do you alms (give gifts to the poor) before men to be seen of them. - **Matthew 6:1**

2. Otherwise ye have no reward of your Father which is in Heaven. - **Matthew 6:1**

3. Therefore when you do your alms do not sound a trumpet, before thee, as the hypocrites do in the synagogues and in the streets, that the may have glory of men. Verily I say unto you, They have their reward. - **Matthew 6:2**

4. But when thou doest alms, let not thy left hand know what thy right hand doeth, Let thy alms (gifts to the poor) be in secret. - **Matthew 6:3,4**

5. And thy Father which seeth in secret himself, shall reward thee openly. - **Matthew 6:4**

6. When thou pray, enter into thy closet. - **Matthew 6:6**

7. Shut the door, pray to thy Father which is in secret. - **Matthew 6:6**

8. And thy Father which seeth in secret shall reward thee openly. - **Matthew 6:6**

9. But when you pray use not vain repetition. - **Matthew 6:7**

10. For your Father knoweth what things ye have need of before you ask him. - **Matthew 6:8**

June 3

JESUS SAID:

1. Pray ye, our Father which art in Heaven. - **Matthew 6:9**

2. Hallowed be thy name. - **Matthew 6:9**

3. Thy kingdom come. - **Matthew 6:10**

4. Thy will be done in earth as it is in Heaven. - Matthew 6:10

5. Give us this day our daily bread. - **Matthew 6:11**

6. And forgive us our debts, as we forgive our debtors. - **Matthew 6:12**

7. And lead us not into temptation. - **Matthew 6:13**

8. But deliver us from evil. - **Matthew 6:13**

9. For thine is the kingdom. - **Matthew 6:13**

10. Thine is the power and the glory, forever, Amen. - **Matthew 6:13**

June 4

JESUS SAID:

1. When thou fastest, anoint thine head, and wash thy face.
   - **Matthew 6:17**

2. That thou appear not unto men to fast but unto thy Father which is in secret. - **Matthew 6:18**

3. And thy Father; which seeth in secret, shall reward thee openly. - **Matthew 6:18**

4. Lay not up for yourselves treasures upon the earth.
   - **Matthew 6:19**

5. Where moth and rust doth corrupt, and where thieves break through and steal. - **Matthew 6:19**

6. But lay up for yourselves treasures in Heaven.
   - **Matthew 6:20**

7. Where neither moth nor rust doth corrupt, and where thieves do not break through and steal. - **Matthew 6:20**

8. For where your treasure is there will your heart be also.
   - **Matthew 6:21**

9. The light of the body is the eye, if therefore thine eye be single thy whole body shall be full of light. - **Matthew 6:22**

10. But if thine eye be evil, thy whole body shall be full of darkness. - **Matthew 6:23**

June 5

JESUS SAID:

1. No man can serve two masters. - **Matthew 6:24**

2. For either he will hate the one and love the other.
   - **Matthew 6:24**

3. Or else he will hold to one and despise the other.
   - **Matthew 6:24**

4. You cannot serve God and mammon. - **Matthew 6:24**

5. Therefore I say unto you, take no thought for your life.
   - **Matthew 6:25**

6. Of what you shall eat, or what ye shall drink. - **Matthew 6:25**

7. Nor yet for your body what ye shall put on. - **Matthew 6:25**

8. Is not the life more than meat, and the body than raiment.
   - **Matthew 6:25**

9. Behold the foul of the air, for they sow not, neither do they reap, nor gather into barns yet your Heavenly Father feedeth them. - **Matthew 6:26**

10. Behold are ye not much better than they? - **Matthew 6:26**

June 6

JESUS SAID:

1. Why take ye thought for raiment. - **Matthew 6:28**

2. Consider the lilies of the field, how they grow; they toil not, neither do they spin. - **Matthew 6:28**

3. And yet I say unto you that even Solomon in all his glory was not arrayed like one of these. - **Matthew 6:29**

4. Wherefore if God so clothe the grass of the field, which today is, and tomorrow is cast into the oven, shall he not much more clothe you. - **Matthew 6:30**

5. O ye of little faith. - **Matthew 6:30**

6. Therefore take no thought saying, what shall we eat? - **Matthew 6:31**

7. Or what shall we drink? - **Matthew 6:31**

8. Or wherewithal shall we be clothed? - **Matthew 6:31**

9. For your Heavenly Father knoweth that ye have need of all these things. - **Matthew 6:32**

10. But seek ye first the kingdom of God, and his righteousness, and all these things shall be added unto you. - **Matthew 6:33**

June 7

JESUS SAID:

1. Take no thought for the morrow. - **Matthew 6:34**

2. For the morrow shall take thoughts for the things of itself.
   - **Matthew 6:34**

3. Sufficient unto the day is the evil thereof. - **Matthew 6:34**

4. And seek not ye what ye shall eat, or what ye shall drink, neither be ye of doubtful mind, your Father knoweth that ye have need of these things what to eat or drink.
   - **Luke 12:29-30**

5. Rather seek ye the kingdom of God. - **Luke 12:31**

6. And all these things shall be added unto you. - **Luke 12:31**

7. Fear not little flock. - **Luke 12:32**

8. For it is your Father's good, pleasure to give you the kingdom.
   - **Luke 12:32**

9. Not every one that saith unto me, Lord, Lord shall enter into the kingdom of Heaven. - **Matthew 7:21**

10. But he that doeth the will of my Father which is in Heaven.
    - **Matthew 7:21**

June 8

JESUS SAID:

1. Therefore all things whatsoever ye would that men should do to you, do ye even so to them. - **Matthew 7:12**

2. This is the law and the prophets. - **Matthew 7:12**

3. Enter ye in at the strait gate. - **Matthew 7:13**

4. For wide is the gate, and broad is the way that leadeth to destruction. - **Matthew 7:13**

5. Many there be which go in there at. - **Matthew 7:13**

6. Because strait is the gate and narrow is the way which leadeth unto life. - **Matthew 7:14**

7. And few there be that find it. - **Matthew 7:14**

8. Beware of false prophets. - **Matthew 7:15**

9. Which come to you in sheep's clothing, but inwardly they are ravening wolves. - **Matthew 7:15**

10. Ye shall know them by their fruits, do men gather grapes of thorns, or figs of thistles? - **Matthew 7:16**

June 9

JESUS SAID:

1. Arise, and be not afraid. - **Matthew 17:7**

2. Verily I say unto you, if ye have faith as a grain of mustard seed, ye shall say unto this mountain, remove hence to yonder place and it shall remove. - **Matthew 17:20**

3. And nothing shall be impossible unto you. - **Matthew 17:20**

4. Howbeit this kind goeth, not out but by prayer and fasting. - **Matthew 17:21**

5. Verily I say unto you, if ye have faith and doubt not, ye shall say unto this mountain, be thou removed, and be thou cast into the sea, it shall be done. - **Matthew 21:21**

6. And all things, whatsoever ye shall ask in prayer believing, ye shall receive. - **Matthew 21:22**

7. Verily I say unto you, have faith, and doubt not. - **Matthew 21:21**

8. Take heed that no man deceive you. - **Matthew 24:4**

9. For many shall come in my name, saying I am Christ. - **Matthew 24:5**

10. And shall deceive many. - **Matthew 24:5**

June 10

JESUS SAID:

1. Verily, verily, I say unto you, he that entereth not by the door into the sheep fold, but climbeth up some other way, the same is a thief and a robber. - **John 10:1**

2. But he that entereth in by the door is the shepherd of the sheep. - **John 10:2**

3. To him the porter openeth and the sheep hear his voice. - **John 10:3**

4. And he calleth his own sheep by name. - **John 10:3**

5. He leadeth them out. - **John 10:3**

6. And when he putteth forth his own sheep, he goeth before them. - **John 10:4**

7. And the sheep follow him; for they know his voice. - **John 10:4**

8. And a stranger will they not follow. - **John 10:5**

9. But they will flee from him. - **John 10:5**

10. For they know not the voice of strangers. - **John 10:5**

June 11

JESUS SAID:

1. Blessed are your eyes, for they see and your ears for they hear. - **Matthew 13:16**
2. For verily I say unto you that many prophets and righteous men have desired to see those things which ye see, and have not seen them. - **Matthew 13:17**
3. And to hear those things which ye hear and have not heard them. - **Matthew 13:17**
4. Hear ye therefore the parable of the sower. - **Matthew 13:18**
5. When anyone heareth the word of the kingdom, and understand it not, then comes the wicked one, and catcheth away that which was sown in his heart. This is he that received seed by the way side.- **Matthew 13:19**
6. But he that received the seed into stony places, the same is he that heareth the word, and anon with joy receiveth it. - **Matthew 13:20**
7. Yet he not root in himself, but dureth for a while; for when tribulation or persecution ariseth because of the word, by and by he is offended. - **Matthew 13:21**
8. He also that received seed among the thorns is he that heareth the word; and the care of this world, and the deceitfulness of riches choke the word, and he becomes unfruitful - **Matthew 13:22**
9. But he that received seed into good ground is he that heareth the word, and understandeth it. - Matthew 13: 23
10. Which also beareth fruit, and bringeth forth, some an hundred -fold, some sixty, some thirty. - **Matthew 13:23**

June 12

JESUS SAID:

1. Ye do err, not knowing the scriptures, nor the power of the God. - **Matthew 22:29**

2. I am the God of Abraham, and the God of Isaac, and the God of Jacob. - **Matthew 22:32**

3. God is not the God of the dead, but of the living. - **Matthew 22:32**

4. Thou shalt love the Lord thy God with all thy heart, and with all thy soul and with all thy mind. - **Matthew 22:37**

5. This is the first and great commandment. - **Matthew 22:38**

6. And the second is like unto it thou shalt love thy neighbor as thyself. - **Matthew 22:39**

7. On these two commandments hang all the law and the prophets. - **Matthew 22:40**

8. What think ye of Christ? Whose son is he? - **Matthew 22:42**

9. Whom do men say that I am? - **Mark 8:27**

10. Whom say ye that I am? - **Mark 8:29**

June 14

JESUS SAID:

1. *Give me to drink.* - **John 4:7**

2. *If thou knewest the gift of God, and who it is that saith to thee, give me to drink, thou wouldest have asked of him, and he would have given thee living water.* - **John 4:10**

3. *Whosoever drinketh of this water shall thirst again.* - **John 4:13**

4. *But whosoever drinketh of the water that I give him shall never thirst.* - **John 4:14**

5. *But the water that I shall give him shall be in him a well of water springing up into everlasting life.* - **John 4:14**

6. *Believe me, the hour cometh when ye shall neither in this mountain, nor yet at Jerusalem worship the Father.* - **John 4:21**

7. *But the hour cometh and now it is when the true worshippers shall worship the Father in spirit and in truth.* - **John 4:23**

8. *For the Father seeketh such to worship him.* - **John 4:23**

9. *God is a Spirit.* - **John 4:24**

10. *They that worship him must worship him in spirit and in truth.* - **John 4:24**

June 14

JESUS SAID:

1. I that speak unto thee am he (the Christ, the Messiah).
   – **John 4:26**

2. Except ye see signs and wonders ye will not believe.
   – **John 4:48**

3. If thou canst believe all things are possible to him that believeth. – **Mark 9:23**

4. I have meat to eat that ye know not of. – **John 4:32**

5. My meat is to do the will of him that sent me, and to finish his work. – **John 4:34**

6. Say not ye there are yet four months, and then cometh harvest? – **John 4:35**

7. Behold, I say unto you lift up your eyes and look on the fields, for they are white already ready to harvest. – **John 4:35**

8. He that reapeth receiveth wages, and gathereth fruit into life eternal. – **John 4:36**

9. That both he that soweth and he that reapeth may rejoice together. – **John 4:36**

10. And herein is that saying true that one soweth and another reapeth. – **John 4:37**

June 15

JESUS SAID:

1. My doctrine is not mine, but his that sent me. - **John 7:16**
2. If any man will do his will, he shall know of the doctrine whether it be of God or whether I speak of myself. - **John 7:17**
3. He that speaketh of himself seeketh his own glory. - **John 7:18**
4. But he that seeketh his glory that sent him, the same is true, and no unrighteousness is in him. - **John 7:18**
5. Did not Moses give the law. - **John 7:19**
6. And yet none of you keepeth the law? - **John 7:19**
7. Judge not according to the appearance, but judge righteous judgements - **John 7:24**
8. If any man thirst, let him come unto me and drink. - **John 7:37**
9. He that believeth on me, as the scripture hath said, out of his belly shall flow rivers of living water. - **John 7:38**
10. If you continue in my word, then are ye my disciples indeed. - **John 8:31**

June 16

JESUS SAID:

1. My sheep hear my voice and I know them and they follow me. - **John 10:27**

2. I give unto them eternal life. - **John 10:28**

3. And they shall never perish. - **John 10:28**

4. Neither shall any man pluck them out of my hand. - **John 10:28**

5. My Father, which gave them me, is greater than all. - **John 10:29**

6. And no man is able to pluck them out of my Father hand. - **John 10:29**

7. Many good works have I shewed you from my Father. - **John 10:32**

8. Is it not written in your law, I said ye are gods? - **John 10:34**

9. If he called them gods unto whom the word of God came, and the scripture cannot be broken. - **John 10:35**

10. Say ye of him, whom the Father hath sanctified, and sent into the world, thou blasphemest because I said, I am the Son of God? - **John 10:36**

June 17

JESUS SAID:

1. He that is not with me is against me. - **Matthew 12:30**

2. And he that gathereth not with me scattereth abroad. - **Matthew 12:30**

3. Wherefore I say unto you, all manner of sin and blasphemy shall be forgiven unto men. - **Matthew 12:31**

4. But the blasphemy against the Holy Ghost shall not be forgiven unto men. - **Matthew 12:31**

5. Whosoever speaketh a word against the Son of man, it shall be forgiven him. - **Matthew 12:32**

6. But whosoever speaketh against the Holy Ghost, it shall not be forgive him, neither in this world, neither in the world to come. - **Matthew 12:32**

7. How can ye being evil, speak good things? - **Matthew 12:34**

8. A good man out of the good treasure of the heart bringeth forth good things. - **Matthew 12:35**

9. And an evil man out of the evil treasure bringeth forth evil things. - **Matthew 12:35**

10. Every idle word that men shall speak they shall give account thereof in the day of judgement for by thy words thou shalt be justified, and condemned. - **Matthew 12:36**-37

June 18

JESUS SAID:

1. Peace be unto you. - **John 20:21,**26

2. As my Father has sent me, even so I send you. - **John 20:21**

3. Receive ye the Holy Ghost. - **John 20:22**

4. Blessed are they that have not seen, and yet believed. - **John 20:29**

5. Come and dine. - **John 21:12**

6. Feed my lambs. - **John 21:15**

7. Feed my sheep. - **John 21:19**

8. Feed my sheep. - **John 21:19**

9. Follow me. - **John 21:19**

10. If I will that he tarry till I come, what is that to thee, follow thou me. - **John 21:22**-23

June 19

JESUS SAID:

1. How hardly shall they that have riches enter into the kingdom of God! - **Mark 10:23**

2. Children, again how hard is it for them that trust in riches to enter into the kingdom of God? - **Mark 10:24**

3. With men it is impossible but not with God. - **Mark 10:27**

4. For with God all things are possible. - **Mark 10:27**

5. Verily I say unto you, there is no man that hath left house, brethren, sisters, father, or mother or wife or children, or lands for my sake, and the gospel's, but he shall receive a hundredfold now in this time, houses, and brethren, and sisters and mothers and children and lands with persecution; and in the world to come eternal life. - **Mark 10:29-30**

6. But many that are first shall be last. - **Mark 10:31**

7. And the last first. - **Mark 10:31**

8. What would ye that I should do for you. - **Mark 10:36**, 51

9. Go thy way, thy faith hath made thee whole. - **Mark 10:52**

10. Have faith in God. - **Mark 11:22**

June 20

JESUS SAID:

1. Swear not at all neither by Heaven; for it is God's throne, nor by earth; for it is his footstool. - **Matthew 5:34**-35

2. Thou shalt not forswear thyself, but shall perform unto the Lord thine oaths. - **Matthew 5:33**

3. Neither shalt thou swear by thy head, because thou cannot make one hair white or black. - **Matthew 5:36**

4. Let your communication be yea, yea, nay, nay; for whatsoever is more than these cometh of evil. - **Matthew 5:37**

5. I say to you resist not evil, but whosoever shall smite thee on thy right cheek, turn to him the other also. - **Matthew 5:39**

6. If any man will sue thee at the law, and take away thy coat, let him have thy cloak also. - **Matthew 5:40**

7. And whosoever shall compel thee to go a mile, go with him two. - **Matthew 5:41**

8. Give to him that asketh thee. - **Matthew 5:42**

9. And from them that would borrow of thee, turn not thou away. - **Matthew 5:42**

10. I say unto you love your enemies. - **Matthew 5:44**

June 21

JESUS SAID:

1. But I say unto you, Love your enemies, bless them that curse you. - **Matthew 5:44**

2. Do good to them that hate you. - **Matthew 5:44**

3. Pray for them that despitefully use you, and persecute you. - **Matthew 5:44**

4. That ye may be the children of your Father which is in Heaven. - **Matthew 5:45**

5. For He maketh his sun to rise on the evil and the good. - **Matthew 5:45**

6. And he sendeth his rain on the just and on the unjust. - **Matthew 5:45**

7. For if ye love them which love you, what reward have ye. - **Matthew 5:46**

8. Do not even the publicans the same. - **Matthew 5:46**

9. If you salute your brother only, (act graciously toward), what do ye more than others. - **Matthew 5:47**

10. Be ye therefore perfect, even as your Father which is in Heaven is perfect. - **Matthew 5:48**

June 22

JESUS SAID:

1. *I will have mercy and not sacrifice.* - **Matthew 9:13**

2. *I am not come to call the righteous, but sinners to repentance.* - **Matthew 9:13**

3. *Be of good comfort, thy faith hath made thee whole.* - **Matthew 9:22**

4. *Believe ye that I am able to do this?* - **Matthew 9:28**

5. *According to your faith be it unto you.* - **Matthew 9:29**

6. *Blessed is he, whosoever shall not be offended in me.* - **Matthew 11:6**

7. *Wisdom is justified of her children.* - **Matthew 11:19**

8. *All things are delivered unto me of my Father.* - **Matthew 11:27**

9. *Come unto me, all ye that labor and are heavy laden, and I will give you rest.* - **Matthew 11:28**

10. *Take my yoke upon you and learn of me; for I am meek, and lowly in heart, and ye shall find rest unto your souls for my yoke is easy, and my burdens is light.* – **Matthew 11:29-30**

June 23

JESUS SAID:

1. My kingdom is not of this world. - **John 18:36**
2. If my kingdom were of this world, then would my servants' fight that I should not be delivered to the Jews. - **John 18:36**
3. But now is my kingdom not from hence. - **John 18:36**
4. Thou sayest that I am King. - **John 18:37**
5. To this end was I born. - **John 18:37**
6. And for this cause came I into the world. - **John 18:37**
7. That I should bear witness unto the truth. - **John 18:37**
8. Everyone that is of truth heareth my voice. - **John 18:37**
9. Thou could have no power at all against me, except it was given thee from above. - **John 19:11**
10. Therefore he that delivered me unto thee hath the greater sin. - **John 19:11**

June 24

JESUS SAID:

1. Suffer it to be so now, for thus it becometh us to fulfil all righteousness. - **Matthew 3:15**

2. It is written, man shall not live by bread alone, but by every word that proceedeth out of the mouth of God. - **Matthew 4:4**

3. It is written, thou shalt not tempt the Lord thy God. - **Matthew 4:7**

4. Get thee hence, Satan, for it is written, thou shalt worship the Lord thy God, and him only shalt thou serve. - **Matthew 4:10**

5. Repent for the kingdom of Heaven is at hand. - **Matthew 4:17**

6. Follow me, I will make you fisher of men. - **Matthew 4:19**

7. Even so every good tree bringeth forth good fruit. - **Matthew 7:17**

8. But a corrupt tree bringeth forth evil fruit. - **Matthew 7:17**

9. A good tree cannot bring forth evil fruit. - **Matthew 7:18**

10. Neither can a corrupt tree bring forth good fruit. - **Matthew 7:18**

June 25

JESUS SAID:

1. Not everyone that saith unto me, Lord, Lord shall enter into the kingdom of Heaven. - **Matthew 7:21**

2. But he that doeth the will of my Father which is in Heaven. - **Matthew 7:21**

3. Many will say unto me, Lord, Lord, have we not prophesied in thy name? - **Matthew 7:22**

4. And in thy name have cast out devils? - **Matthew 7:22**

5. And in thy name done many works? - **Matthew 7:22**

6. And then will I profess unto them, I never knew you. - **Matthew 7:23**

7. Depart from me, you who work iniquity. - **Matthew 7:23**

8. Therefore, whosoever hear these sayings of mine and doeth them, I will liken him unto a wise man, which built his house upon a rock. - **Matthew 7:24**

9. The rain descended and the flood came, and the wind blew, and beat upon the house and it fell not because it was founded upon a rock. - **Matthew 7:25**

10. Everyone that heareth these sayings of mine, and doeth them not, shall be liken to a foolish man which built his house upon the sand, and the rain descended, the floods came and that house, fell and great was the fall of it. - **Matthew 7:26-27**

June 26

JESUS SAID:

1. All power is given unto me in Heaven and in earth.
   - **Matthew 28:18**

2. Go ye therefore, and teach all nations. - **Matthew 28:19**

3. Baptizing them in the name of the Father, and of the Son, and of the Holy Ghost. - **Matthew 28:19**

4. Teaching them to observe all things whatsoever I have commanding you. - **Matthew 28:20**

5. And lo, I am with you always, even unto the end of the world. Amen - **Matthew 28:20**

6. He that believeth and is baptized shall be saved. - **Mark 16:16**

7. But he that believeth not shall be damned. - **Mark 16:16**

8. And these signs shall follow them that believe; In my name they shall cast out devils. - **Mark 16:17**

9. They shall speak with new tongues. - **Mark 16:17**

10. They shall take up serpents; and if they drink any deadly thing, it shall not hurt them, they shall lay hands on the sick, and they shall recover. - **Mark 16:18**

June 27

JESUS SAID:

1. Lo I am with you always, even unto the end of the world. Amen - **Matthew 28:20**

2. Seest thou these great buildings? - **Mark 13:2**

3. There shall not be left one stone upon another, that shall not be thrown down. - **Mark 13:2**

4. Take heed lest any man deceive you. - **Mark 13:5**

5. For many shall come in my name, saying, I am Christ; and shall deceive many. - **Mark 13:6**

6. And when ye shall hear of wars and rumors of wars, be ye not troubled. - **Mark 13:7**

7. For such things must needs be; but the end shall not be yet. - **Mark 13:7**

8. For nations shall rise against nations and kingdoms against kingdoms. - **Mark 13:8**

9. And there shall be earthquakes in divers places. - **Mark 13:8**

10. And there shall be famines and troubles; these are the beginnings of sorrows. - **Mark 13:8**

June 28

JESUS SAID:

1. Take heed to yourselves for they shall deliver you up to the councils. - **Mark 13:9**

2. And in the synagogues ye shall be beaten. - **Mark 13:9**

3. And ye shall be brought before rulers and kings for my sake. - **Mark 13:9**

4. And the gospel must first be published among all nations. - **Mark 13:10**

5. But when they shall lead you, and deliver you up, take no thought beforehand what ye shall speak. - **Mark 13:11**

6. Neither do ye premeditate. - **Mark 13:11**

7. But whatsoever shall be given you in that hour, that speak ye. - **Mark 13:11**

8. For it is not ye that speak, but the Holy Ghost. - **Mark 13:11**

9. Now brother shall betray the brothers to death, and the father the son, the children shall rise up against their parents and shall cause them to be put to death. - **Mark 13:12**

10. And ye shall be hated of all men for my sake, but he that shall endure unto the end, the same shall be saved. - **Mark 13:13**

June 29

JESUS SAID:

1. Then shall many be offended and shall betray one another. - **Matthew 24:10**

2. And shall hate one another. - **Matthew 24:10**

3. And many false prophets shall arise, and shall deceive many. - **Matthew 24:11**

4. And because iniquity shall abound, the love of many shall wax cold. - **Matthew 24:12**

5. But he that shall endure unto the end, the same shall be saved. - **Matthew 24:13**

6. And this gospel of the kingdom shall be preached in all the world for a witness unto all nations, and then shall the end come. - **Matthew 24:14**

7. When ye therefore shall see the abomination of desolation, spoken by Daniel, the prophet, stand in the holy place. - **Matthew 24:15**

8. Then let them that be in Judea flee to the mountain. - **Matthew 24:16, Luke 21:21**

9. When ye shall see Jerusalem compassed with armies, then know that the desolation thereof is nigh. - **Luke 21:20**

10. Let them that are in the midst of it depart out and let not them that are in the countries enter thereinto. - **Luke 21:,21**

June 30

JESUS SAID:

1. For these be the days of vengeance, that all things which are written may be fulfilled. - **Luke 21:22**

2. But woe to them that are with child, and to them that give suck, in those days. - **Luke 21:23**

3. For there shall be a great distress in the land, and wrath up on this people. - **Luke 21:23**

4. Let him which is on the housetop not come down to take anything out of his house. - **Matthew 24:17**

5. Neither let him which is the field return back to take his clothes. - **Matthew 24:18**

6. But pray ye that your flight be not in winter, neither on the Sabbath day, for then shall be great tribulation, such as was not since the beginning of the world to his time, no, nor ever shall be. - **Matthew 24:20-21**

7. And except those days should be shortened, there should no flesh be saved. - **Matthew 24:22**

8. But for the elect's sake those days shall be shorten. - **Matthew 24:22**

10. And they shall fall by the edge of the sword, and shall be led away captive into all nations, and Jerusalem shall be trodden down of the Gentiles, until the times of the Gentiles be fulfilled. - **Luke 21:24**

July 1

JESUS SAID:

1. Then if any man shall say unto you, lo here is Christ, or there; believe it not. - **Matthew 24:23**

2. For there shall arise false Christ's, and false prophets, and shall shew great signs and wonders . - **Matthew 24:24**

3. Insomuch that, if it were possible, they shall deceive and seduce the very elect. - **Matthew 24:24)**

4. But take ye heed, behold I have foretold you all things. - **Matthew 24:25**

5. Wherefore if they shall say unto you, behold, he is in the desert, go not forth. - **Matthew 24:26**

6. If they shall say unto you, behold, he is in the secret chambers; believe it not. - **Matthew 24:26**

7. For as the lightning comes out of the east, and shineth even unto the west, so shall the coming of the Son of man be. - **Matthew 24:27**

8. But in those days, after that tribulation, the sun shall be darkened. - **Mark 13:24**

9. And the moon shall not give her light. - **Mark 13:24**

10. And the stars of Heaven shall fall, and the powers that are in Heaven shall be shaken. - **Mark 13:25**

July 2

JESUS SAID:

1. For wheresoever the carcase is, there will the eagles be gathered together. - **Matthew 24:28**

2. The powers of the Heavens shall be shaken. - **Matthew 24:29; Luke 21:26**

3. And upon the earth distress of nations, with perplexity. - **Luke 21:25**

4. The sea and the waves roaring. - **Luke 21:25**

5. Men's hearts failing them for fear, and for looking after those things which are coming on the earth. - **Luke 21:26**

6. And then shall appear the sign of the Son of man in Heaven. - **Matthew 24:30**

7. And then shall all the tribes of the earth mourn. - **Matthew 24:30**

8. And the shall they see the Son of man coming in the clouds of Heaven with power and great glory. - **Matthew 24:30**

9. And then shall he send his angels, with a great sound of a trumpet. - **Matthew 24:31**

10. And they shall gather together his elect from the force winds, from the uttermost part of the earth to the uttermost part of Heaven. - **Mark 13:27**

July 3

JESUS SAID:

1. Now learn a parable of the fig tree. - **Matthew 24:32; Mark 13:28**

2. Behold the fig tree, and all the trees. - **Luke 21:29**

3. When they now shoot forth and when his branch is yet tender, and putteth forth leaves, ye know that summer is near. - **Matthew 24:32; Luke 21:30**

4. So likewise ye, when ye see these things, know that it is near, even at the doors. - **Matthew 24:33, Mark 13:29**

5. Verily, I say unto you, this generation shall not pass away tell all these things be done and fulfilled. - **Matthew 24:34**

6. Heaven and earth shall pass away, but my words shall not pass away. – **Matthew 24:35; Mark 13:31; Luke 21:33**

7. But of that day and hour knoweth no man, no, not the angels which are in Heaven, neither the Son but my Father only. - **Matthew 24:36; Mark 13:32**

8. Take heed watch and pray. - **Mark 13:33**

9. For you know not when the time is. - **Mark 13:33**

10. Take heed to yourselves, lest at any time your heart be overcharged with surfeiting, and drunkenness and care of this life, and so that day comes upon you unaware. - **Luke 21:34**

July 4

JESUS SAID:

1. But as the days of Noah were, so shall also the coming of the Son of man be. - **Matthew 24:37**
2. For as the days that were before the flood they were eating and drinking, marrying and given in marriage until the day that Noe entered into the ark. - **Matthew 24:38**
3. And knew not until the flood came, and took them all away. - **Matthew 24:39**
4. So shall the coming of the Son of man be. - **Matthew 24:39**
5. Then shall two be in the field; the one shall be taken, and the other left. - **Matthew 24:40**
6. Two women shall be grinding at the mill; the one shall be taken, and the other left. - **Matthew 24:41**
7. Likewise also as it was in the days of Lot, they did eat, they drank, they bought, they sold, they planted, they build. - **Luke 17:28**
8. But the same day Lot went out of Sodom at rained fire and brimstone from the Heaven, and destroyed them all. - **Luke 17:29**
9. Watch therefore, for ye know not what hour your Lord doth come. - **Matthew 24:42**
10. Take heed, watch ye therefore and pray for ye know not when the time is. - **Mark 13:33**

July 5

JESUS SAID:

1. But know this, that if the good man of the house had known in what watch the thief would come, he would have watched.
   - **Matthew 24:43**

2. And would have not suffered his house to be broken up.
   - **Matthew 24:43**

3. For the Son of man is as a man taking a far journey, who left his house, and gave authority to his servants, and to every man his work and commanded the porter to watch.
   - **Mark 13:34**

4. Watch ye therefore, for you know not when the Master of the house cometh, at even, or at midnight, or at the cock crowing, or in the morning. - **Mark 13:35**

5. Lest coming suddenly he find you sleeping. - **Mark 13:36**

6. And what I say unto you, I say unto all, watch. - **Mark 13:37**

7. For as a snare shall it come on all them that dwell on the face of the whole earth. - **Luke 21:35**

8. Therefore be ye also ready. - **Matthew 24:44**

9. For in such an hour as you think not the Son of man cometh.
   - **Matthew 24:44**

10. Who then is a faithful and wise servant whom his Lord hath made ruler over his household, to give them meat in due season. - **Matthew 24:45**

July 6

JESUS SAID:

1. Blessed is the servant whom his Lord when he cometh shall find as doing. - **Matthew 24:46**

2. Verily I say unto you, that he shall make him ruler over all his goods. - **Matthew 24:47**

3. But and if that evil servant shall say in his heart, my Lord delayeth his coming. - **Matthew 24:48**

4. And begin to smite his fellow servants. - **Matthew 24:49**

5. And to eat and drink with the drunken. - **Matthew 24:49**

6. The Lord of that servant shall come in a day when he looketh not for him. - **Matthew 24:50**

7. And in an hour that he is not aware of. - **Matthew 24:50**

8. And shall cut him asunder and appoint him his portion with the hypocrites. - **Matthew 24:51**

9. There shall be weeping and gnashing of teeth. - **Matthew 24:51**

10. Watch ye therefore, and pray always, that ye may be accounted worthy to escape all these things that shall come to pass, and to stand before the Son of man. - **Luke 21:36**

July 7

JESUS SAID:

1. Then shall the kingdom of Heaven be likened unto ten virgins. - **Matthew 25:1**

2. Which took their lamps and went forth to meet the bridegroom. - **Matthew 25:1**

3. And five of them were wise and five were foolish. - **Matthew 25:2**

4. They that were foolish took their lamps and took no oil with them. - **Matthew 25:3**

5. But the wise took oil their vessels with their lamps. - **Matthew 25:4**

6. While the bridegroom tarried they all slumbered and slept. - **Matthew 25:5**

7. And at midnight there was a cry made. - **Matthew 25:6**

8. Behold, the bridegroom cometh, go ye out to meet him. - **Matthew 25:6**

9. Then all those virgin's arose, and trimmed their lamps. - **Matthew 25:7**

10. And the foolish said unto the wise, give us of your oil, for our lamps are gone out. - **Matthew 25:8**

July 8

JESUS SAID:

1. But the wise virgin answered, saying not so. - **Matthew 25:9**
2. The wise virgins answered, lest there be not enough for us and you. - **Matthew 25:9**
3. The wise answered but go ye rather to them that sell and buy for yourselves. - **Matthew 25:9**
4. And while they went to buy, the bridegroom came. - **Matthew 25:10**
5. And they that were ready went in with him to the marriage; and the door was shut. - **Matthew 25:10**
6. Afterwards came also the other virgins, saying, Lord, Lord, open to us. - **Matthew 25:11**
7. But he answered, and said, verily I say unto you, I know you not. - **Matthew 25:12**
8. When once the Master of the house is risen up, and hath shut to the door, and ye begin to stand without and to knock at the door, saying Lord, Lord, open unto us; and he shall answer and say unto you, I know you not whence ye are. - **Luke 13:25**
9. Watch therefore, for ye know neither the day nor the hour wherein the Son of man cometh. - **Matthew 25:13**
10. Strive to enter in at the strait gate, for many, I say unto you, will seek to enter in, and shall not be able. - **Luke 13:24**

July 9

JESUS SAID:

1. And so he that receiveth five talents came and brought other five talents. - **Matthew 25:20**
2. Saying Lord thou deliveredst unto me five talents and behold, I have gained beside them five talents more. - **Matthew 25:20**
3. The Lord said unto him well done, thou good and faithful servant. - **Matthew 25:21**
4. Thou hast been faithful over a few things, I will make thee ruler over many things. **Matthew 25:21**
5. Enter thou into the joy of thy Lord. - **Matthew 25:21**
6. He also that had received two talents came and said, Lord thou deliveredst unto me two talents beside them. - **Matthew 25:22**
7. His Lord said unto him, well done, good and faithful servant; thou hast been faithful servant; thou hast been faithful over a few things. - **Matthew 25:23**
8. Enter thou into the joy of thy Lord. - **Matthew 25:23**
9. Then he which had received the one talent came and said, Lord I knew thee, that thou are a hard man, reaping where thou hast not sown, and gathering where thou hast not strawed; and I was afraid, and went and hid thy talent in the earth, lo there thou hast; that is thine. - **Matthew 25:24-25**
10. His Lord answered and said unto him, Thou wicked and slothful servant, thou knewest that I reap where I sowed not and gathered where I have not strawed. - **Matthew 25:26**

July 10

JESUS SAID:

1. Thou oughtest therefore to have put my money to the exchanges then at my coming should have received mine own with usury(interest). - **Matthew 25:27**
2. Take therefore the talent from him and give it unto him which hath ten talents. - **Matthew 25:28**
3. For unto everyone that hath shall be given, and he shall have abundance; but from him that hath not shall be taken away even that which he hath. - **Matthew 25:29**
4. And cast ye the unprofitable servant into outer darkness; there shall be weeping and gnashing of teeth.
   - **Matthew 25:30**
5. A certain nobleman went into a far country to receive for himself a kingdom and to return. - **Luke 19:12**
6. And he called his ten servants and delivered them ten pounds, and said unto them, occupy till I come. - **Luke 19:13**
7. But the citizens hated him and sent a message after him, saying, we will not have this man to reign over us.
   - **Luke 19:14**
8. And it came to pass, that when he was returned, having received the kingdom. - **Luke 19:15**
9. Then he commanded these servants to be called unto him, to whom he had given the money. - **Luke 19:15**
10. That he might know how much every man had gained by trading. - **Luke 19:15**

July 11

JESUS SAID:

1. Then came the first saying Lord, thy pound hath gained ten pounds. - **Luke 19:16**

2. And he said unto him, well, thou good servant. - **Luke 19:17**

3. Because thou hast been faithful in a very little, have thou authority over ten cities. - **Luke 19:17**

4. And the second came, saying Lord, thy pound has gained five pounds. - **Luke 19:18**

5. Likewise to him, be thou also over five cities. - **Luke 19:19**

6. And another came saying Lord, behold, here is thy pound, which I have kept laid up in a napkin. - **Luke 19:20**

7. He said, for I feared thee, because thou art an austere man, thou takest up that thou layedst not down, and reapest what thou didst not sow. - **Luke 19:21**

8. Unto him, out of thine own mouth will I judge thee thou wicked servant. - **Luke 19:22**

9. Thou knew I was an austere man, taking up that I laid not down and reaping what I did not sow. - **Luke 19:22**

10. Wherefore then gavest not my money unto the bank, that at my coming might have received mine own with usury. - **Luke 19:23**

July 12

JESUS SAID:

1. And he said unto them that stood by; Take from him the pound and give it to him that hath ten pounds. - **Luke 19:24**

2. And they said unto him, Lord, he hath ten pounds. - **Luke 19:25**

3. For I say unto you, That unto every one which hath shall be given. - **Luke 19:26**

4. And from him that hath not, even that he hath shall be take from him. - **Luke 19:26**

5. But those mine enemies which would not that I should reign over them,bring hither, and slay them before me. - **Luke 19:27**

6. A certain man planted a vineyard, and let it forth to husbandmen, and went into a far country for a long time. - **Luke 20:9**

7. And at the season he sent a servant to the husbandmen, that they should give him of the fruit of the vineyard. - **Luke 20:10**

8. But the husbandmen beat him and sent him away empty. - **Luke 20:10**

9. And again he sent another servant; and they beat him also, and entreated him shamefully, and sent him away empty. - **Luke 20:11**

10. And again he sent a third, and they wounded him also, and cast him out. - **Luke 20:12**

July 13

JESUS SAID:

1. Then said the Lord of the vineyard, what shall I do?
   - **Luke 20:13**
2. I will send my beloved son; it may be they will reverence him when they see him. - **Luke 20:13**
3. But when the husbandmen saw him, they reasoned among themselves, saying, this is the heir, come, let us kill him. That the inheritance may be ours. - **Luke 20:14**
4. What therefore shall the Lord of the vineyard do unto them.
   - **Luke 20:15**
5. He shall come and destroy these husbandmen, and shall give the vineyard to others. - **Luke 20:16**
6. What is this then that is written, the stone which the builders rejected, the same is become the head of the corner?
   - **Luke 20:17**
7. Whosoever shall fall upon that stone shall be broken.
   - **Luke 20:18**
8. But on whomsoever it shall fall, it will grind him to powder. - **Luke 20:18**
9. When the Son of man shall come in his glory, and all the holy angels with him, then shall he sit upon the throne of his glory. - **Matthew 25:31**
10. And before him shall be gathered all nations. - **Matthew 25:32**

July 14

JESUS SAID:

1. And he shall separate them one from another, as a shepherd divideth his sheep from the goats. - **Matthew 25:32**

2. And he shall set the sheep on his right hand, but the goats on the left. - **Matthew 25:33**

3. Then shall the King say unto them on his right hand, Come, ye blessed of my Father. - **Matthew 25:34**

4. Inherit the kingdom prepared for you from the foundation of the world. - **Matthew 25:34**

5. For I was hungered and ye gave me meat. - **Matthew 25:35**

6. I was thirsty, and you gave me drink. - **Matthew 25:35**

7. I was a stranger, and ye took me in. - **Matthew 25:35**

8. Naked, and ye clothed me. - **Matthew 25:36**

9. I was sick and ye visited me. - **Matthew 25:36**

10. I was in prison, and ye came unto me. - **Matthew 25:36**

July 15

JESUS SAID:

1. Then shall the righteous answer him, saying Lord, when saw we thee hungered, and fed thee? Or thirsty, and gave thee drink ? **Matthew 25:37**
2. The righteous answered, when saw we thee a stranger; and took thee in? Or naked, and clothed thee? - **Matthew 25:38**
3. The righteous answered, or when saw we thee sick, or in prison, and came unto thee? - **Matthew 25:39**
4. And the King shall answer and say unto them, verily I say unto you, inasmuch as ye are done it unto one of the least of these my brethren, ye have done it unto me. - Matthew 25:40
5. Then shall he say also unto them on the left hand depart from me, ye cursed, into everlasting fire, prepared for the devil & his angels. - **Matthew 25:41**
6. For I was an hungered and ye gave me no meat. - **Matthew 25:42**
7. I was thirsty and ye gave me no drink. - **Matthew 25:42**
8. I was a stranger and you took me not in, naked and you clothed me not .. - **Matthew 25:43**
9. Sick and in prison, and ye visited me not. - **Matthew 25:43**
10. Then they also answered him, saying Lord, when saw we thee an hungered or athirst, or a stranger, or naked, or sick, or in prison and did not minister unto thee? Then shall he answer them saying, Verily I say unto you, Inasmuch as ye did it not to one of the least of these, ye did it not to me. - Matthew 25:44-45

July 16

JESUS SAID:

1. For the kingdom of Heaven is as a man traveling into a far country, who called his own servants and delivered unto them his goods. - **Matthew 25:14**

2. Unto one he gave five talents. - **Matthew 25:15**

3. To another two. - **Matthew 25:15**

4. To another one. - **Matthew 25:15**

5. To every man according to his several ability. - **Matthew 25:15**

6. And straightway took his journey. - **Matthew 25:15**

7. Then he that received the five talents went and traded with the same, and made them other five talents. - **Matthew 25:16**

8. Likewise he that had received two he also gained other two. - **Matthew 25:17**

9. But he that received one, went and digged in the earth and hid his Lord's money. - **Matthew 25:18**

10. After a long time the Lord of those servants cometh and reckoneth with them. - **Matthew 25:19**

July 17

JESUS SAID:

1. Verily I say unto you, inasmuch as ye did it not to one of the least of these, ye did it not to me. - **Matthew 25:45**
2. And these shall go away into everlasting punishment but the righteous into life eternal. - **Matthew 25:46**
3. Who then is that faithful and wise steward, whom his Lord shall make ruler over his household, to give them their portion of meat in due season? - **Luke 12:42**
4. Blessed is that servant whom his Lord when he cometh shall find so doing. - **Luke 12:43**
5. Of a truth I say unto you, that he will make him ruler over all that he hath. - **Luke 12:44**
6. But and if that servant say in his heart, my Lord delayeth his coming; and shall begin to beat the menservants and maidens, and to eat and drink, and to be drunken. - **Luke 12:45**
7. The Lord of that servant will come in a day when he looketh not for him. - **Luke 12:46**
8. And at an hour when he not aware, and will cut him in sunder, and will appoint him his portion with the unbelievers. - **Luke 12:46**
9. And that servant, which knew his Lord's will, and prepared not himself, neither did according to his will, shall be beaten with many stripes. - **Luke 12:47**
10. But he that knew not, and did commit things worthy of stripes shall be beaten with few stripes. - **Luke 12:48**

July 18

JESUS SAID:

1. For unto whomsoever much is given, of him shall be much required. - **Luke 12:48**

2. And to whom men have committed much, of him they will ask more. - **Luke 12:48**

3. I am come to send fire on the earth; and what will I if it be already kindled? - **Luke 12:49**

4. But I have a baptism to be baptized with; and how am I straitened till it be accomplished! - **Luke 12:50**

5. Suppose ye that I am come to give peace on earth? - **Luke 12:51**

6. I tell you nay; but rather division. - **Luke 12:51**

7. For from henceforth there shall be five in one house divided, three against two and two against three. - **Luke 12:52**

8. The father shall be divided against the son, and the son against the father. - **Luke 12:53**

9. The mother against the daughter, and the daughter against the mother. - **Luke 12:53**

10. The mother in law against the daughter in law, and the daughter in law, against hermother in law. - **Luke 12:53**

July 19

JESUS SAID:

1. When ye see a cloud rise out of the west, straightway ye say, there cometh a shower, and so it is. - **Luke 12:54**

2. And when ye see the south wind blow, ye say, there will be heat; and it cometh to pass. - **Luke 12:55**

3. Ye hypocrites, ye can discern the face of the sky and of the earth. - **Luke 12:56**

4. But how is it that ye do not discern this time? - **Luke 12:56**

5. When it is evening ye say, it will be fair weather for the sky is red. - **Matthew 16:2**

6. And in the morning, it will be foul weather today, for the sky is red and lowering. - **Matthew 16:3**

7. O ye hypocrites, ye can discern the face of the sky but can ye not discern the sign of the times. - **Matthew 16:3**

8. Yea, and why even of yourselves judge ye not what is right. - **Luke 12:57**

9. A wicked and adulterous generation seeketh after a sign. - **Matthew 16:4**

10. And there shall no sign be given unto it, but the sign of the prophet Jonas. – **Matthew 16:4**

July 20

JESUS SAID:

1. When thou goest with thine adversary to the magistrate, as thou are in the way, give diligence that thou mayest be delivered from him. - **Luke 12:58**
2. Lest he hale thee to judge. - **Luke 12:58**
3. And the judge deliver thee to the officer, and the officer cast thee into prison. - Luke 12:58
4. I tell thee, thou shall not depart thence, till thou hast the paid the very last mite. - **Luke 12:59**
5. Suppose ye that these Galilaeans were sinners above all the Galileans, because they suffered such things? - **Luke 13:2**
6. I tell you nay; but except ye repent, ye shall all likewise perish. - **Luke 13:3**
7. Or those eighteen upon which the tower in Siloam fell and slew them, think ye that they were sinners above all men that dwell in Jerusalem? - **Luke 13:4**
8. I tell you nay; but, except ye repent ye shall all likewise perish. - **Luke 13:5**
9. A certain man had a fig tree planted in his vineyard; and he came and sought fruit thereon and found none. - **Luke 13:6**
10. Then he said to the dresser of his vineyard; behold these three years I come seeking fruit on this fig tree and find none; cut it down; why cumbereth it the ground? - **Luke 13:7**

July 21

JESUS SAID:

1. And he answering him said unto him, Lord let it alone this year, also, till I shall dig about it and dung it. - **Luke 13:8**

2. And if it bare fruit well; and if not, then after that thou shall cut it down. - **Luke 13:9**

3. No man eat fruit of thee hereafter forever. - **Mark 11:14**

4. Ye shall know them by their fruits. - **Matthew 7:16**

5. Do men gather grapes of thorns, or figs of thistles? - **Matthew 7:16**

6. Even so every good tree bringeth forth good fruit. - **Matthew 7:17**

7. But a corrupt tree, bringeth forth evil fruit. - **Matthew 7:17**

8. A good tree cannot bring forth evil fruit, neither can a corrupt tree bring forth good fruit. - **Matthew 7:18**

9. Every tree that bringeth not forth good fruit is hewn down, and cast into the fire. - **Matthew 7:19**

10. Wherefore by their fruits ye shall know them. - **Matthew 7:20**

July 22

JESUS SAID:

1. Suffer it to be so now; for thus it becometh us to fulfil all righteousness. - **Matthew 3:15**

2. It is written, man shall not live by bread alone, but by every word that proceedeth out of the mouth of God.
   - **Matthew 4:4**; **Luke 4:4**

3. It is written again, thou shalt not tempt the Lord thy God.
   - **Matthew 4:7**; **Luke 4:12**

4. Get thee hence, Satan; for it is written, thou shalt worship the Lord thy God, and him only shalt thou serve.
   - **Matthew 4:10**; **Luke 4:8**

5. Repent; for the kingdom of Heaven is at hand. - **Matthew 4:17**

6. The time is fulfilled, and the kingdom of God is at hand; repent ye, and believe the gospel - **Mark 1:15**

7. The Spirit of the Lord is upon me, because he hath anointed me to preach the gospel to the poor; - **Luke 4:18**

8. He hath sent me to heal the broken hearted. - **Luke 4:18**

9. To preach deliverance to the captive. - **Luke 4:18**

10. And the recovering of sight to the blind, to set at liberty them that are bruised. And to preach the acceptable year of the Lord. - **Luke 4:18**, 19

July 23

JESUS SAID:

1. *Follow me, and I will make you fishers of men.* - **Matthew 4:19**
2. *Come ye after me, and I will make you to become fisher of men.* - **Mark 1:17**
3. *He has sent me to preach the acceptable year of the Lord.* - **Luke 4:19**
4. *This day is this scripture fulfilled in your ears.* - **Luke 4:21**
5. *What seek ye.* - **John 1:38**
6. *Come and see.* - **John 1:39**
7. *I am the light of the world : he that follows me shall not walk in darkness but shall have the light of life* - **John 8:12**
8. *Though I bear record of myself.* - **John 8:14**
9. *Yet my record is true.* - **John 8:14**
10. *For I know whence I came, and whither I go; but ye cannot tell whence I come, and whither I go.* - **John 8:14**

July 24

JESUS SAID:

1. *I am the light of the world.* - **John 8:12**

2. *Ye judge after the flesh, I judge no man.* - **John 8:15**

3. *For if I judge, I am not alone, but I and the Father that sent me.* - **John 8:16**

4. *It is also written in your law, that the testimony of two men is true.* - **John 8:17**

5. *I am one that bear witness of myself, and the Father that sent me beareth witness for me.* - John 8:18

6. *Ye neither know me, nor my Father.* - **John 8:19**

7. *If ye had known me, ye should have known my Father also.* - **John 8:19**

8. *I go my way, and ye shall seek me, and shall die in your sins.* - **John 8:21**

9. *Whither I go, ye cannot come.* - **John 8:22**

10. *Ye are from beneath, I am from above, ye are of this world, I am not of this world.* - **John 8:23**

July 25

JESUS SAID:

1. I said therefore unto you, that ye shall die in your sins; for if ye believe not that I am he, ye shall die in your sins.
   – **John 8:24**

2. Even the same that I said unto you from the beginning. – **John 8:25**

3. I have many things to say and to judge of you.
   – **John 8:26**

4. But he that sent me is true. – **John 8:26**

5. And I speak to the world those things which I have heard of him. – **John 8:26**

6. When ye have lifted up the Son of man, then shall ye know that I am he. – **John 8:28**

7. And that I do nothing of myself. – **John 8:28**

8. But as my Father with taught me, I speak these things.
   – **John 8:28**

9. And he that sent me is with me. – **John 8:29**

10. The Father hath not left me alone for I do always those things that please him. – **John 8:29**

July 26

JESUS SAID:

1. *If ye continue in my word, then are ye my disciples indeed.*
   - **John 8:31**

2. *And ye shall know the truth, and the truth shall make you free.* - **John 8:32**

3. *Ye shall be made free.* - **John 8:33**

4. *Verily, verily, I say unto you, whosoever committeth sin is the servant of sin.* - **John 8:34**

5. *And the servant abideth not in the house forever, but the Son abideth ever.* - **John 8:35**

6. *If the Son therefore shall make you free, ye shall be free indeed.* - **John 8:36**

7. *I know ye are Abraham's seed; but ye seek to kill me, because my word hath no place in you.* - **John 8:37**

8. *I speak that which I have seen with my Father.* - **John 8:38**

9. *And ye do that which ye have seen with your father.*
   - **John 8:38**

10. *If ye were Abraham's children, ye would do the work of Abraham.* - **John 8:39**

July 27

JESUS SAID:

1. But now ye seek to kill me, a man that hath told you the truth, which I have heard of God; this did not Abraham. - **John 8:40**

2. Ye do the deeds of your father. - **John 8:41**

3. If God were you Father, you would love me. - **John 8:42**

4. For I proceeded forth and came from God. - **John 8:42**

5. Neither came I of myself, but he sent me. - **John 8:42**

6. Why do ye not understand my speech? - **John 8:43**

7. Even because ye cannot hear my word. - **John 8:43**

8. Ye are of your father the devil, and the lusts of your father ye will do. - **John 8:44**

9. He was a murderer from the beginning and abode not in truth, because there is no truth in him. - **John 8:44**

10. When he speaketh a lie, he speaketh of his own, for he is a liar, and the father of it. - **John 8:44**

July 28

JESUS SAID:

1. And because I tell you the truth, ye believe me not. **– John 8:45**

2. Which of you convinceth me of sin. **– John 8:46**

3. And if I say the truth do ye not believe me. **– John 8:46**

4. He that is of God heareth God's word. **– John 8:47**

5. Ye therefore hear them not, because ye are not of God. **– John 8:47**

6. I have not a devil, but I honor my Father, and ye do dishonor me. **– John 8:49**

7. And I seek not mine own glory. **– John 8:50**

8. There is one that seeketh and judgeth. **– John 8:50**

9. Verily, verily, I say unto you, if a man keep my saying, he shall never see death. **– John 8:51**

10. If a man keep my saying, he shall never taste of death. **– John 8:52**

July 29

JESUS SAID:

1. *If I honor myself my honor is nothing.* - **John 8:54**

2. *It is my Father that honoureth me, of whom ye say that he is your God.* - **John 8:54**

3. *Yet ye have not known him, but I know him.* - **John 8:55**

4. *And if I should say I know him not, I shall be a liar like unto you.* - **John 8:55**

5. *But I know him and keep his saying.* - **John 8:55**

6. *Your father Abraham rejoiced to see my day, and he saw it and was glad.* - **John 8:56**

7. *Verily, verily, I say unto you, before Abraham was, I am.* - **John 8:58**

8. *Verily, verily, I say unto you, the Son can do nothing of himself, but what he seeth the Father do.* - **John 5:19**

9. *For what things soever he doeth, these also doeth the Son likewise.* - **John 5:19**

10. *For the Father loveth the Son, and sheweth him all things that himself doeth; and he will shew him greater works than these that ye may marvel.* - **John 5:20**

July 30

JESUS SAID:

1. For as the Father raiseth up the dead, and quickeneth them; even so the Son quickeneth whom he will. - **John 5:21**
2. For the Father judgeth no man, but hath committed all judgement unto the Son. - **John 5:22**
3. That all men should honor the Son, even as they honor the Father. - **John 5:23**
4. He that honoureth not the Son honoureth not the Father which hath sent him. - **John 5:23**
5. Verily, verily, I say unto you, he that heareth my word, and believe on him that sent me, hath everlasting life, and shall not come into condemnation. - **John 5:24**
6. But is passed from death unto life. - **John 5:24**
7. Verily, verily, I say unto you, the hour is coming, and now is when the dead shall hear the voice of the Son of God, and they that hear shall live. - **John 5:25**
8. For as the Father hath life in himself, so hath he given to the Son to have life in himself. - **John 5:26**
9. And he hath given him authority to execute judgement also, because he is the Son of man. - **John 5:27**
10. Marvel not at this, for the hour is coming in which all that are in the graves shall hear his voice. - **John 5:28**

July 31

JESUS SAID:

1. All that are in the graves shall hear his voice and shall come forth; they that have done good, unto the resurrection of life. - **John 5: 28,29**

2. And they that have done evil, unto the resurrection of damnation. - **John 5:29**

3. I can of mine own self do nothing. - **John 5:30**

4. As I hear, I judge. - **John 5:30**

5. And my judgement is just. - **John 5:30**

6. Because I seek not mine own will. - **John 5:30**

7. But I seek the will of the Father which hath sent me. - **John 5:30**

8. If I bear witness of myself, my witness is not true. - **John 5:31**

9. There is another that beareth witness of me. - **John 5:32**

10. And I know that the witness which he witnesseth of me is true. - **John 5:32**

August 1

JESUS SAID:

1. Ye sent unto John and He bare witness unto the truth.
   - **John 5:33**

2. But I receive not testimony from man, but these things I say, that ye might be saved. - **John 5:34**

3. John was a burning and a shining light. - **John 5:35**

4. And ye were willing for a season to rejoice in his light.
   - **John 5:35**

5. But I have a greater witness than that of John . - **John 5:36**

6. For the works which the Father hath given me to finish the same works that I do, bear witness of me, that the Father hath sent me. - **John 5:36**

7. And the Father himself which hath sent me, hath bore witness of me. - **John 5:37**

8. Ye have neither heard his voice at any time, nor seen his shape. - **John 5:37**

9. And ye, have not his word abiding in you. - **John 5:38**

10. For whom he hath sent, him you believe not. - **John 5:38**

August 2

JESUS SAID:

1. Search the scriptures, for in them ye think ye have eternal life. - **John 5:39**

2. And they are they which testify of me. - **John 5:39**

3. And ye will not come to me, that ye might have life. - **John 5:40**

4. I receive not honor from men. - **John 5:41**

5. But I know you, that ye have not the love of God in you. - **John 5:42**

6. I am come in my Father's name, and you receive me not. - **John 5:43**

7. If another shall come in his own name, him ye will receive. - **John 5:43**

8. How can ye believe, which receive honor one of another and seek not the honor that cometh from God only? - **John 5:44**

9. Do not think that I will accuse you to the Father. - **John 5:45**

10. There is one that accuseth you, even Moses, in whom you trust. - **John 5:45**

August 3

JESUS SAID:

1. For had you believed Moses, ye would have believed me, for he wrote of me. - **John 5:46**
2. But if ye believe not his writing, how shall ye believe my words?- **John 5:47**
3. If they hear not Moses and the prophets, neither will they be persuaded, though one rose from the dead. - **Luke:16:31**
4. Not everyone that saith unto me Lord, Lord shall enter into the kingdom of Heaven. - **Matthew 7:21**
5. Many will say to me in that day, Lord, Lord, have we not prophesied in thy name? And in thy name have cast out devils? - **Matthew 7:22**
6. And in thy name have done many wonderful works? - **Matthew 7:22**
7. And then I will profess unto them, I never knew you, depart from me, ye that work iniquity. - **Matthew 7:23**
8. Therefore, whosoever heareth these sayings of mine, and doeth them, I will liken him unto a wise man, which built his house upon a rock. - **Matthew 7:24**
9. And every one that heareth them not shall be likened unto a foolish man which builds his house upon the sand. - **Matthew 7:26**
10. And the rain descended and the floods came, and the winds blew, and beat upon that house and it fell and great was the fall of it. - **Matthew 7:27**

August 4

JESUS SAID:

1. The spirit of the Lord is upon me. - **Luke 4:18**
2. Because he hath anointed me to preach the gospel to the poor. - **Luke 4:18**
3. He hath sent me to heal the brokenhearted. - **Luke 4:18**
4. To preach deliverance to the captives. - **Luke 4:18**
5. And recovering of sight to the blind. - **Luke 4:18**
6. To set at liberty them that are bruised. - **Luke 4:18**
7. To preach the acceptable year of the Lord. - **Luke 4:19**
8. This day is this scripture fulfilled in your ears. - **Luke 4:21**
9. Ye will surely say unto me, this proverb, physician heal thyself. - **Luke 4:23**
10. Verily I say of you, no prophet is accepted in his own country. - **Luke 4:24**

August 5

JESUS SAID:

1. A prophet is not without honor, save in his own country, and in his own house and among his own kin. - **Matthew 13:57; Mark 6:4; Luke 4:24**

2. But I tell you the truth many widows were in Israel in the days of Elias, when the Heavens was shut up three years and six months when great famine was throughout all the land. - **Luke 4:25**

3. But unto none of them was Elias sent, save unto Sarepta a city of Sidon, unto a woman that was a widow. - **Luke 4:26**

4. And many lepers were in Israel at the time of Eliseus, the prophet, and none of them was cleaned, saving Naaman, the Syrian. - **Luke 4:27**

5. I must preach the kingdom of God to other cities also, for therefore am I sent. - **Luke 4:43**

6. Hold thy peace, and come out of him. - **Luke 4:35**

7. I will be thou clean. - **Matthew 8:3**

8. I will come and heal him. - **Matthew 8:7**

9. Verily I say unto you, I have not found so great faith, no not in Israel. - **Matthew 8:10**

10. And I say unto you many shall come from the east and west, and shall sit down with Abraham, and Isaac, and Jacob, in the kingdom of Heaven. - **Matthew 8:11**

August 6

JESUS SAID:

1. Repent; for the kingdom of Heaven is at hand. - **Matthew 4:17**
2. As ye go, preach saying the kingdom of Heaven is at hand. - **Matthew 10:7**
3. After this manner therefore pray ye; our Father which art in Heaven, hallowed be thy name, thy kingdom come, thy will be done in earth, as it is in Heaven. Give us this day our our daily bread . And forgive us our debts as we forgive our debtors and lead us not into temptation but deliver us from evil; for thine is the kingdom, and the power, and the glory, forever. Amen. - **Matthew 6:9**-13
4. Pray ye therefore the Lord of the harvest, that he will send forth labourers into his harvest. - **Matthew 9:38**
5. The kingdom of Heaven is like to a grain of mustard seed, which a man took and sowed in his field. - **Matthew 13:31**
6. Which is the least of all seed; but when it is grown it is the greatest among herbs and becometh a tree, so that the birds in the air come in and lodge in the branches thereof. - **Matthew 13:32**
7. The kingdom of Heaven is like unto leaven, which a woman took, and hid in three measures of meal, till the whole was leavened. - **Matthew 13:33**
8. So is the kingdom of God, as if a man should cast seed into the ground. - **Mark 4:26**
9. And he should sleep, and rise night and day, and the seed should spring up and grow up, he knoweth not how. - **Mark 4:27**
10. For the earth bringeth forth fruit of herself, first the blade, then the ear, after that the full corn in the ear. - **Mark 4:28**

August 7

JESUS SAID:

1. I must preach the kingdom of God in cities also, for therefore am I sent. - **Luke 5:43**

2. Verily, verily, I say unto thee; except a man be born again, he cannot see the Kingdom of God. - **John 3:3**

3. Verily, verily, I say unto thee, except a man be born of water and the spirit he cannot enter into the Kingdom of God. - **John 3:5; Mark 16:16**

4. That which is born of the flesh is flesh. - **John 3:6**

5. That which is born of spirit is spirit. - **John 3:6**

6. Marvel not that I said unto thee, ye must be born again. - **John 3:7**

7. The wind bloweth where it listeth, and thou hearest the sound thereof, but canst not tell whence it cometh, and whither it goeth. - **John 3:8**

8. So is everyone that is born of the Spirit. - **John 3:8**

9. My kingdom is not of this world. - **John 18:36**

10. Thou sayest that I am a king. - **John 18:37**

August 8
JESUS SAID:

1. If my kingdom were of this world, then would my servants fight, that I should not be delivered to the Jews, but now is my kingdom not from hence. - **John 18:36**
2. Art thou a Master of Israel and knowest not these things? - **John 3:10**
3. Verily, verily, I say unto thee, we speak that we do know, and testify that we have seen; and ye receive not our witness. - **John 3:11**
4. If I have told you earthly things, and ye believe not, how shall ye believe, if I tell you of Heavenly things? - **John 3:12**
5. And no man hath ascended up to Heaven, but he that came down from Heaven, even the Son of man which is in Heaven. - **John 3:13**
6. And as Moses lifted up the serpent in the wilderness, even so must the Son of man be lifted up. - **John 3:14**
7. That whosoever believeth in him should not perish but have eternal life. - **John 3:15**
8. For God so loved the world that he gave his only begotten Son. - **John 3:16**
9. That whosoever believeth in him should not perish, but have everlasting life. - John 3:16
10. For God sent not his Son into the world to condemn the world; but that the world through him might be saved. - **John 3:17**

August 9

JESUS SAID:

1. He that believeth on him is not condemned, but he that believeth not is condemned already. - **John 3:18**

2. Because he hath not believed in the name of the only begotten Son of God. - **John 3:18**

3. And this is the condemnation, that the light is come into the world, and men loved darkness rather than light. - **John 3:19**

4. Because their deeds were evil. - **John 3:19**

5. For everyone that doeth evil, hateth the light. - **John 3:20**

6. Neither cometh them to the light, lest his deeds should be reproved. - **John 3:20**

7. But he that doeth truth cometh to the light, that his deeds may be made manifest. - **John 3:21**

8. That they are wrought in God. - **John 3:21**

9. The scribes and the Pharisees sit in Moses seat. - **Matthew 23:2**

10. All therefore whatsoever they bid you observe, that observe and do, but do not ye after their works, for they say and do not. - **Matthew 23:3**

August 10

JESUS SAID:

1. The scribes and the Pharisees, they bind heavy burdens and grievous to be borne and lay them on men's shoulders.
   - **Matthew 23:4**

2. But they themselves will not move them with one of their fingers. - **Matthew 23:4**

3. But all their works they do for to be seen of men.
   - **Matthew 23:5**

4. They make broad their phylacteries, and enlarge the borders of their garments. - **Matthew 23:5**

5. And they love the uppermost rooms at feast and the chief seats in the synagogues. - **Matthew 23:6**

6. And they love greetings in the markets, and to be called of men, Rabbi, Rabbi. - **Matthew 23:7**

7. But be not ye called Rabbi, for one is your Master, even Christ, and all ye are brethren. - **Matthew 23:8**

8. And call no man your father upon the earth. - **Matthew 23:9**

9. For one is your Father, which is in Heaven. - **Matthew 23:9**

10. Neither be ye called master; for one is your Master even Christ. - **Matthew 23:10**

August 11

JESUS SAID:

1. But he that is greatest among you shall be your servant.
   – **Matthew 23:11**
2. And whosoever shall exalt himself shall be abased.
   – **Matthew 23:12**
3. And he that shall humble himself shall be exalted.
   – **Matthew 23:12**
4. But woe unto you, scribes and Pharisees, hypocrites ! for you shut up the kingdom of Heaven against men. – **Matthew 23:13**
5. For ye neither go in yourselves, neither suffer ye them that are entering to go in. – **Matthew 23:13**
6. Woe to you scribes and Pharisees, hypocrites; for ye devour your widows' houses. – **Matthew 23:14**
7. And for a pretence make long prayer; therefore ye shall receive the greater damnation. – **Matthew 23:14**
8. Woe to you, scribes and Pharisees, hypocrites, for ye compass sea and land to make one proselyte. – **Matthew 23:15**
9. And when he is made, ye make him twofold more the child of hell than yourselves. – **Matthew 23:15**
10. Woe unto you, ye blind guides, which say, whosoever shall swear by the temple it is nothing; but whosoever shall swear by the gold of the temple, he is a debtor. – **Matthew 23:16**

August 12

JESUS SAID:

1. Ye fools and blind; for whether is greater, the gold or the temple that sanctifieth the gold? - **Matthew 23:17**
2. Whosoever shall swear by the altar, it is nothing; but whosoever sweareth by the gift, that is upon it, he is guilty. - **Matthew 23:18**
3. Ye fools and blind; for whether is greater, the gift, or the altar which sanctifieth the gift? - **Matthew 23:19**
4. Whosoever therefore shall swear by the altar, sweareth by it, and by all things thereon. - **Matthew 23:20**
5. And whoso shall swear by the temple, sweareth by it and by him that dwelleth therein. - **Matthew 23:21**
6. And he that shall swear by Heaven, sweareth by the throne of God, and by him that sitteth thereon. - **Matthew 23:22**
7. Woe to you scribes and Pharisees, hypocrites! For ye pay tithe of mint and anise and cummin, and have omitted the weightier matters of the law, judgement, mercy, and faith. - **Matthew 23:23**
8. These ought ye to have done, and not leave the other undone. - **Matthew 23:23**
9. Ye blind guides, which strain at a gnat and swallow a camel. - **Matthew 23:24**
10. Woe to you scribes and Pharisees, hypocrites! For ye make clean the outside of the cup, and of the platter, but within they are full of extortion and excess. – **Matthew 23:25**

August 13

JESUS SAID:

1. Thou blind Pharisee cleanse first that which is within the cup and platter that the outside of them may be clean also. – **Matthew 23:26**
2. Woe unto you scribes and Pharisees, hypocrites! For ye are like unto whited sepulchres which indeed appear beautiful outward but are within full of dead men's bones, and of all uncleanness. – **Matthew 23:27**
3. Even so ye also outwardly appear righteous unto men, but within ye are full of hypocrisy and iniquity. – **Matthew 23:28**
4. Woe, unto you scribes and Pharisee, hypocrites! Because ye build the tombs of the prophets, and garnish the sepulchres of the righteous. – **Matthew 23:29**
5. And say, if we had been in the days of our fathers, we would not have been partakers with them in the blood of the prophets. – **Matthew 23:30**
6. Wherefore ye be witnesses unto yourselves, that ye are the children of them that killed the prophets. – **Matthew 23:31**
7. Fill ye up then the measure of your fathers. – **Matthew 23:32**
8. Ye serpents, ye generation of vipers, how can ye escape the damnation of hell? – **Matthew 23:33**
9. Wherefore behold, I send unto you prophets, wise men, and scribes. – **Matthew 23:34**
10. And some of them ye shall kill and crucify; and some of them shall ye scourge in your synagogues, and persecute them from city to city. – **Matthew 23:34**

August 14

JESUS SAID:

1. That upon you may come all the righteous blood shed upon the earth. - **Matthew 23:35**

2. From the blood of the righteous Abel unto the blood of Zacharias son of Barachias, whom you slew between the temple and the alter. - **Matthew 23:35**

3. Verily, I say unto you all these things shall come upon this generation. - **Matthew 23:36**

4. O Jerusalem, Jerusalem, thou that killest the prophets, and stonest them which are sent unto thee. - **Matthew 23:37**

5. How often would I have gathered thy children together. - **Matthew 23:37**

6. Even as a hen gathereth her chicken under her wings, and ye would not. - **Matthew 23:37**

7. Behold your house is left unto you desolate. - **Matthew 23:38**

8. For I say unto you, ye shall not see me henceforth, till ye shall say, Blessed is he that cometh in the name of the Lord. - **Matthew 23:39**

9. See ye not all these things? - **Matthew 24:2**

10. Verily I say unto you. There shall not be left here one stone upon another that shall not be thrown down. - **Matthew 24:2**

August 15

JESUS SAID:

1. Take heed that no man deceive you. - **Matthew 24:4**

2. For many shall come, saying I am Christ, and shall deceive many. - **Matthew 24:5**

3. Take heed and beware of the leaven of the Pharisees and the Sadducees. - **Matthew 16:6**

4. O ye of little faith why reason ye among yourselves because ye have brought no bread? - **Matthew 16:8**

5. Do ye not understand neither remember, the five loaves and the five thousand and how many baskets ye took up. - **Matthew 16:9**

6. Neither the seven loaves of the four thousand, and how many baskets ye took up. - **Matthew 16:10**

7. How is it that ye do not understand that I spake it not to you concerning bread, that ye should beware of the leaven of the Pharisees and of the Sadducees? - **Matthew 16:11**

8. Whom do men say that, I the Son of man am? - **Matthew 16:13**

9. But whom say ye that I am? - **Matthew 16:15**

10. Blessed art thou Simon Barjona, for flesh and blood hath not revealed it unto thee but my Father which is in Heaven. - **Matthew 16:17**

August 16

JESUS SAID:

1. And I say also unto thee; thou are Peter, and upon this rock I will build my church. - **Matthew 16:18**
2. And the gates of hell shall not prevail against it. - **Matthew 16:18**
3. And I will give unto thee the keys of the kingdom of Heaven. - **Matthew 16:19**
4. And whatever thou shalt bind on earth, shall be bound in Heaven. - **Matthew 16:19**
5. And whatever thou shalt loose on earth shall be loosed in Heaven. - **Matthew 16:19**
6. The Son of man must suffer many things, and be rejected of the elders and chief priest and scribes, and be slain and be raised the third day. - **Luke 9:22**
7. If any man will come after me, let him deny himself, and take up his cross daily, and follow me. - **Luke 9:23, Matthew 16:24**
8. For whosoever will save his life shall lose it. - **Matthew 16:25, Luke 9:23**
9. But whosoever will lose his life for my sake, the same shall save it - **Luke 9:24**; (shall find it). - **Matthew 16:25**
10. What is man profited if he shall gain the whole world and lose his own soul, or what shall a man give in exchange for his soul - **Matthew 16:26**.(or be cast away). – **Luke 9:25**

August 17

JESUS SAID:

1. For whosoever shall be ashamed of me and of my words, of him shall the Son of man be ashamed. - **Luke 9:26**

2. When he shall come in his own glory. - **Luke 9:26**

3. And in his Father's. - **Luke 9:26**

4. And of the holy angels. - **Luke 9:26**

5. For the Son of man shall come in the glory of his Father, with his angels. - **Matthew 16:27**

6. And then he shall reward every man according to his works. - **Matthew 16:27**

7. Verily, I say unto you, there be some standing here, which shall not taste of death. - **Matthew 16:28**

8. Till they see the Kingdom of God. - **Luke 9:27**

9. Till they see the Son of man coming in his Kingdom. - **Matthew 16:28**

10. Arise, and be not afraid. - **Matthew 17:7**

August 18

JESUS SAID:

1. When it is evening, ye say, it will be fair weather for the sky is red. - **Matthew 16:2**

2. And in the morning it will be foul weather to-day for the sky is red and lowering. - **Matthew 16:3**

3. O' ye hypocrites, ye can discern the face of the sky; but can ye not discern the signs of the times? - **Matthew 16:3**

4. A wicked and adulterous generation seeketh after a sign. - **Matthew 16:4**

5. And there shall no sign be given unto it, but the sign of the prophet Jonas. - **Matthew 16:4**

6. Why doth this generation seek after a sign? - **Mark 8:12**

7. Verily I say unto you. There shall no sign be given unto this generation. - **Mark 8:12**

8. Except ye see signs and wonders, ye will not believe. - **John 4:48**

9. Go thy way; thy son liveth. - **John 4:50**, 53

10. Wilt thou be made whole? - **John 5:6**

August 19

JESUS SAID:

1. Rise, take up thy bed and walk. - **John 5:8, 11**

2. Behold, thou art made whole. - **John 5:14**

3. Sin no more. - **John 5:14**

4. Lest a worse things come unto thee. - **John 5:14**

5. My Father worketh hitherto, and I work. - **John 5:17**

6. Verily, verily I say unto you, the Son can do nothing of himself, but what he seeth the Father do. - **John 5:19**

7. For what he seeth the Father do; for what things soever he doeth. - **John 5:19**

8. These also doeth the Son likewise. - **John 5:19**

9. For the Father loveth the Son, and sheweth him all things that himself doeth. - **John 5:20**

10. And he will shew him greater works than these, that ye may marvel. - **John 5:20**

August 20

JESUS SAID:

1. For as the Father raiseth up the dead, and quickeneth them. - **John 5:21**

2. Even so the Son quickeneth whom he will. - **John 5:21**

3. For the Father judgeth no man, but hath committed all judgement unto the Son. - **John 5:22**

4. Judge not, that ye be not judge. - **Matthew 7:1; Luke 6:37**

5. For with what judgement ye judge, ye shall be judged. - **Matthew 7:2**

6. And with what measure ye mete, it shall be measured to you again. - **Matthew 7:2**

7. And why beholdest thou the mote that is in thy brother's eye. - **Matthew 7:3**

8. But considerest not the beam that is in thine own eye. - **Matthew 7:3**

9. Or how wilt thou say to thy brother, let me pull out the mote of thine eye. - **Matthew 7:4**

10. And behold, a beam is in thine own eye? - **Matthew 7:4**

August 21

JESUS SAID:

1. Thou hypocrite, first cast out the beam out of thine own eye. – **Matthew 7:5**

2. And then shalt thou see clearly to cast out the mote out of thy brother's eye. – **Matthew 7:5**

3. Judge not, and ye shall not be judged ; Condemn not, and ye shall not be condemned. – **Luke 6:37**

4. Forgive, and ye shall be forgiven. – **Luke 6:37**

5. Give, and it shall be given unto you, good measure, pressed down, and shaken together and running over shall men give unto you bosom. – **Luke 6:38**

6. For with the same measure that ye mete, withal it shall be measured to you, again. – **Luke 6:38**

7. But I say unto you which hear. – **Luke 6:27**

8. Love your enemies. – **Luke 6:27**

9. Do good to them which hate you. – **Luke 6:27**

10. Bless them that curse you. – **Luke 6:28**

August 22

JESUS SAID:

1. Pray for them which despitefully use you. - **Luke 6:28**

2. And to him that smiteth thee on the one cheek offer also the other. - **Luke 6:29**; **Matthew 5:39**

3. And him that taketh away thy cloak, forbid not to take thy coat also. - **Luke 6:29**

4. But I say unto you, that ye resist not evil. - **Matthew 5:39**

5. And if any man will sue thee at the law, and take away the coat, let him have thy cloak also. - **Matthew 5:40**

6. But I say unto you, Love your enemies,bless them that curse you,do good to them that hate you,and pray for them which despitefully use you, and persecute you. - **Matthew 5:44**

7. And whosoever shall compel thee to go a mile, go with him twain. - **Matthew 5:41**

8. Give to him that asketh thee and from him that would borrow of thee, turn thou not away. - **Matthew 5:42**

9. Of him that taketh away thy goods ask them not again. - **Luke 6:30**

10. And as ye would that men should do to you, do ye also to them likewise. - **Luke 6:31**

August 23

JESUS SAID:

1. That ye may be the children of your Father which is in Heaven; for he maketh his sun to rise on the evil and on the good, and sendeth rain on the just and the unjust.
   – **Matthew 5:45**

2. For if ye love them which love you, what thank have you?
   – **Luke 6:32–Matthew 5:46**

3. For sinners also love those that love them. – **Luke 6:32**

4. For if ye love them that love you, what reward have ye?
   – **Matthew 5:46**

5. Do not even the publicans the same. – **Matthew 5:46**

6. And if ye salute your brethren only, what do ye more than others? – **Matthew 5:47**

7. Do not even the publicans so? – **Matthew 5:47**

8. And if you do good to them which do good to you, what thanks have ye. – **Luke 6:33**

9. For sinners also do even the same. – **Luke 6:33**

10. And if ye lend to them of whom ye hope to receive, what thanks have ye? – **Luke 6:34**

August 24

JESUS SAID:

1. For sinners also lend to sinners, to receive as much again. – **Luke 6:34**

2. But love ye your enemies and do good. – **Luke 6:35**

3. And do good, and lend, hoping for nothing again. – **Luke 6:35**

4. And your reward shall be great. – **Luke 6:35**

5. And ye shall be the children of the Highest. – **Luke 6:35**

6. For he is kind unto the unthankful and to the evil. – **Luke 6:35**

7. Be ye therefore merciful, as your Father also is merciful. – **Luke 6:36**

8. Be ye therefore perfect. – **Matthew 5:48**

9. As your Father which is in Heaven perfect. – **Matthew 5:48**

10. Take heed that ye do not your alms before men, to be seen of them. – **Matthew 6:1**

August 25

JESUS SAID:

1. Take heed that you do not your alms before men,, to be seen of them: otherwise you have no reward of your Father which is in Heaven. - **Matthew 6:1**
2. Therefore when thou doest thine alms, do not sound a trumpet before thee. - **Matthew 6:2**
3. As the hypocrites do in the synagogues, and in the streets that they may have glory of men. - **Matthew 6:2**
4. Verily I say unto you, they have their reward. - **Matthew 6:2**
5. But when thou doest alms, let not thy left hand know what thy right hand doeth. - **Matthew 6:3**
6. That thine alms may be in secret. - **Matthew 6:4**
7. And thy Father which seeth in secret himself shall reward thee openly. - **Matthew 6:4**
8. When thou makest a dinner or a supper, call not thy friends, nor thy brethren, neither thy kinsmen, nor thy rich neighbors, lest they also bid thee again and a recompense be made thee. - **Luke 14:12**
9. But when thou makest a feast, call the poor, the maimed, the lame, the blind. - **Luke 14:13**
10. And thou shalt be blessed, for they cannot recompense thee, for thou shalt be recompensed at the resurrection of the just. - **Luke 14:14**

August 26

JESUS SAID:

1. A certain man made a great supper, and bade many.
   – **Luke 14:16**
2. And sent his servant at supper time to say to them that were bidden, Come, for all things are now ready. – **Luke 14:17**
3. And they all with one consent began to make excuse.
   – **Luke 14:18**
4. The first said unto him, I have bought a piece of ground, and I must needs go and see it, I pray thee have me excused.
   – **Luke 14:18**
5. And another said, I have bought five yoke of oxen, and I go to prove them; I pray thee have me excused. – **Luke 14:19**
6. And another said, I have married a wife, and therefore I cannot come. – **Luke 14:20**
7. So that servant came, and shewed his lord these things.
   – **Luke 14:21**
8. Then the master of the house being angry said to his servant, go out quickly into the streets and lanes of the city, and bring in hither the poor, and the maimed, and the halt, and the blind. – **Luke 14:21**
9. And the servant said, lord, it is done as thou hast commanded, and yet there is room. – **Luke 14:22**
10. And the lord said unto the servant, go out into the highways and hedges and compel them to come in, that my house may be filled. – **Luke 14:23**

August 27

JESUS SAID:

1. For I say unto you, that none of those men which were bidden shall taste of my supper. - **Luke 14:24**

2. For the kingdom of Heaven is like unto a man that is an householder, which went out early in the morning to hire laborers into his vineyard. - **Matthew 20:1**

3. And when he had agreed with the laborers for a penny a day he sent them into his vineyard. - **Matthew 20:2**

4. And he went out about the third hour, and saw others standing idle in the marketplace. - **Matthew 20:3**

5. And he said unto them; go ye also unto the vineyard, and whatsoever is right, I will give you. And they went their way. - **Matthew 20:4**

6. Again he went out the sixth, and the ninth hour, and did likewise. - **Matthew 20:5**

7. And about the eleventh hour, he went out and found others standing idle. - **Matthew 20:6**

8. And he saith unto them, why stand ye here all day idle? - **Matthew 20:6**

9. They said, unto him, because no man hath hired us. - **Matthew 20:7**

10. He saith unto them, go ye also into the vineyard, and whatsoever is right, that shall ye receive. - **Matthew 20:7**

August 28

JESUS SAID:

1. So when even was come, the lord of the vineyard saith unto his steward, call the labourers, and give them their hire, beginning from the last unto the first. - **Matthew 20:8**
2. And when they came that were hired about the eleventh hour, they received every man a penny. - **Matthew 20:9**
3. But when the first came, they supposed that they should have received more. - **Matthew 20:10**
4. And they likewise received every man a penny. - **Matthew 20:10**
5. And when they received it they murmured against the good man of the house - **Matthew 20:11**
6. Saying, these last have wrought but one hour, and thou hast made them equal unto us, which have borne the burden and heat of the day. - **Matthew 20:12**
7. But he answered one of them, and said, friend, I do the no wrong; didst not thou agree with me for a penny? - **Matthew 20:13**
8. Take that thine is, and go thy way: I will give unto this last, even as unto thee. - **Matthew 20:14**
9. Is it not lawful for me to do what I will with mine own? Is thine eye evil because I am good? - **Matthew 20:15**
10. So the last shall be first, and the first last, for many be called, but few chosen. - **Matthew 20:16**

August 29
JESUS SAID:

1. When thou art bidden of any man to a wedding, sit not down in the highest room, lest a more honorable man than thou be bidden of him. - **Luke 14:8**

2. And he that bade thee and him come and say to thee, give this man place, and thou begin with shame to take the lowest room. - **Luke 14:9**

3. But when thou art bidden, go and sit down in the lowest room. - **Luke 14:10**

4. That when he that bade thee cometh, he may say unto thee friend, go up higher. - **Luke 14:10**

5. Then shalt thou have worship in the presence of them that sit at meat with thee. - **Luke 14:10**

6. For whosoever exalteth himself shall be abased (humbled). - **Luke 14:11**

7. And he that humbleth himself, shall be exalted. - **Luke 14:11**

8. But many that are first shall be last, and the last shall be first. - **Matthew 19:30**

9. The kingdom of Heaven is like unto a certain king, which made a marriage for his son. - **Matthew 22:2**

10. And sent forth his servants to call them that were bidden to the wedding and they would not come. - **Matthew 22:3**

August 30

JESUS SAID:

1. Again the king sent forth other servants, saying, tell them which are bidden, behold I have prepared my dinner; my oxen and my fatlings are killed and all things are ready: come unto the marriage. - **Matthew 22:4**

2. But they made light of it, and went their ways, one to his farm, another to his merchandise. - **Matthew 22:5**

3. And the remnant took his servants and entreated (handled) them spitefully, and slew them. - **Matthew 22:6**

4. But when the king heard thereof, he was wroth. - **Matthew 22:7**

5. And the king sent forth his armies, and destroyed those murderers, and burned up their city. - **Matthew 22:7**

6. The king said to his servants, the wedding is ready, but they which were bidden were not worthy. - **Matthew 22:8**

7. Go ye therefore into the highway, and as many as ye shall find, bid to the marriage. - **Matthew 22:9**

8. So the servants went out into the highways and gathered together all as many as they found .

9. Both bad and good. - **Matthew 22:10**

10. And the wedding was furnished with guest. - **Matthew 22:10**

August 31

JESUS SAID:

1. When the king came in to see the guest, he saw there a man which had not a wedding garment. - **Matthew 22:11**

2. And he saith unto him, friend, how camest thou in hither not having a wedding garment? - **Matthew 22:12**

3. And he was speechless. - **Matthew 22:12**

4. Then said the king to the servants, bind his hand and foot and take him away, and cast him into outer darkness.
   - **Matthew 22:13**

5. There shall be weeping and gnashing of teeth.
   - **Matthew 22:13**

6. For many are called, but few are chosen. - **Matthew 22:14**

7. Verily, I say unto you, there is no man that hath left house, or parents or brethren, or wife, or children for the kingdom of God's sake. - **Luke 18:29**

8. Who shall not receive manifold more in this present time, and in the world to come, life everlasting. - **Luke 18:30**

9. But the children of the kingdom shall be cast out into outer darkness; there shall be weeping and gnashing of teeth.
   - **Matthew 8:12**

10. Go thy way and as thou hast believed, so be it done unto thee.
    - **Matthew 8:13**

September 1

JESUS SAID:

1. Every kingdom divided against itself is brought to desolation.
   - **Matthew 12:25**

2. And every city or house divided against itself cannot stand.
   - **Matthew 12:25**

3. And if Satan cast out Satan, he is divided against himself.
   - **Matthew 12:26**

4. How then shall his kingdom stand ? - **Matthew 12:26**

5. And if I by Beelzebub cast out devils, by whom do your children cast them out. - **Matthew 12:27**

6. Therefore, they shall be your judges. - **Matthew 12:27**

7. But if I cast out devils by the Spirit of God, then the kingdom of God is come unto you. - **Matthew 12:28**

8. Or else how can one enter into a strong man's house, and spoil his goods. - **Matthew 12:29**

9. Except he first bind the strongman. - **Matthew 12:29**

10. And then he will spoil his house. - **Matthew 12:29**

September 2

JESUS SAID:

1. He that is not with me is against me. - **Matthew 12:30**

2. And he that gathereth not with me scattereth abroad. - **Matthew 12:30**

3. Wherefore I say unto you, all manner of sin and blasphemy shall be forgiven unto men. - **Matthew 12:31**

4. But blasphemy against the Holy Ghost shall not be forgiven unto men. - **Matthew 12:31**

5. And whosoever speaketh a word against the Son of man, it shall be forgiven him. - **Matthew 12:32**

6. But whosoever speaketh against the Holy Ghost, it shall not be forgiven him, neither in this world neither in the world to come. - **Matthew 12:32**

7. Either make the tree good and his fruit good, or else make the tree corrupt and his fruit corrupt. - **Matthew 12:33**

8. For a tree is known by his fruit. - **Matthew 12:33**

9. O' generation of vipers, how can ye, being evil speak good things. - **Matthew 12:34**

10. For out of the abundance of the heart the mouth speaketh. - **Matthew 12:34**

September 3

JESUS SAID:

1. A good man out of the good treasure of the heart bringeth forth good things. - **Matthew 12:35**

2. And an evil man out of the evil treasure bringeth forth evil things. - **Matthew 12:35**

3. For a good tree bringeth not forth corrupt fruit. - **Luke 6:43**

4. Neither doth a corrupt tree brings forth good fruit. - **Luke 6:43**

5. For every tree is known by his own fruit. - **Luke 6:44**

6. For of thorns men do not gather figs, nor of a bramble bush, gather they grapes. - **Luke 6:44**

7. A good man, out of the good treasure of his heart bringeth forth that which is good. - **Luke 6:45**; **Matthew 12:35**

8. And an evil man, out of the evil treasures of his heart bringeth forth that which is evil. - **Luke 6:45**; **Matthew 12:35**

9. For of the abundance of the heart his mouth speaketh. - **Luke 6:45**

10. And why call ye me, Lord, Lord, and do not the things which I say ? - **Luke 6:46**

September 4

JESUS SAID:

1. But I say unto you, that every idle word that men shall speak, they shall give account thereof in the day of judgement.
   - **Matthew 12:36**

2. For by thy words, thou shalt be justified. - **Matthew 12:37**

3. And by thy words thou shalt be condemned. - **Matthew 12:37**

4. And why call ye me Lord, Lord and do not the things which I say? - **Luke 6:46**

5. Whosoever cometh to me, and heareth my sayings, and doeth them, I will shew you to whom he is like. - **Luke 6:47**

6. He is like a man which builds a house, and digged deep, and laid the foundation on a rock. - **Luke 6:48**

7. And when flood arose the stream beat vehemently upon the house and could not shake it. - **Luke 6:48**

8. For it was founded upon a rock. - **Luke 6:48**

9. But he that heareth and doeth not, is like a man that without a foundation, build a house upon the earth. - **Luke 6:49**

10. Against which the stream did beat vehemently and immediately it fell, and the ruin of the house was great.
    - **Luke 6:49**

September 5

JESUS SAID:

1. An evil and adulterous generation seeketh after a sign.
   - **Matthew 12:39**

2. And there shall no sign be given to it, but the sign of the prophet Jonas. - **Matthew 12:39**

3. For as Jonas was three days and three nights in the whale's belly. - **Matthew 12:40**

4. Shall the Son of man be three days and three nights in the heart of the earth. - **Matthew 12:40**

5. The men of Nineveh shall rise in judgement with this generation. - **Matthew 12:41**

6. And shall condemn it. - **Matthew 12:41**

7. Because they repented at the preaching of Jonas.
   - **Matthew 12:41**

8. And behold, a greater than Jonas is here. - **Matthew 12:41**

9. The queen of the south shall rise up in the judgement with this generation, and shall condemn it, for she came from the uttermost parts of the earth to hear the wisdom of Solomon.
   - **Matthew 12:42**

10. And behold, a greater than Solomon is here. - **Matthew 12:42**

September 6

JESUS SAID:

1. When the unclean spirit is gone out of a man, he walketh through dry places, seeking rest, and findeth none.
   - **Matthew 12:43; Luke 11:24**
2. Then he saith, I will return into my house from whence I came out. - **Matthew 12:44**
3. And when he is come, he findeth it empty, swept and garnished. - **Matthew 12:44; Luke 11:25**
4. Then goeth he, and taketh with him seven other spirits more wicked than himself, and they enter in and dwell there.
   - **Matthew 12:45**
5. And the last state of that man is worse than the first.
   - **Matthew 12:45; Luke 11:26**
6. Even so shall it be also unto this wicked generation.
   - **Matthew 12:45**
7. But if I with the finger of God, cast out devils, no doubt the kingdom of God is come upon you. - **Luke 11:20**
8. When a strong man armed keepeth his palace, his goods are peace. - **Luke 11:21**
9. But when a stronger than he comes upon him, and overtake him, he taketh from him all his armour, wherein he trusted, and divide his spoils. - **Luke 11:22**
10. He that is not with me is against me, and he that gathereth not with me scattered abroad. - **Matthew 12:30**

September 7

JESUS SAID:

1. Yea rather, blessed are they that hear the word of God, and keep it. - **Luke 11:28**

2. The fox have holes, and the birds of the air have nest. - **Matthew 8:20**

3. But the Son of man hath not where to lay his head. - **Matthew 8:20**

4. Follow me. - **Matthew 8:22**

5. Let the dead bury their dead. - **Matthew 8:22**

6. Why are ye fearful, a' ye of little faith. - **Matthew 8:26**

7. Go. - **Matthew 8:32**

8. Son, be of good cheer; thy sins be forgiven thee. - **Matthew 9:2**

9. Wherefore think ye evil in your hearts? - **Matthew 9:4**

10. For whether is easier to say, thy sins be forgiven thee; or to say arise, and walk? - **Matthew 9:5**

September 8

JESUS SAID:

1. But that ye may know that the Son of man hath power on earth to forgive sins. - **Matthew 9:6**

2. Arise, take up thy bed, and go unto thine house. - **Matthew 9:6**

3. Follow me. - **Matthew 9:9**

4. They that be whole need not a physician, but they that are sick. - **Matthew 9:12**

5. But go ye and learn what that meaneth. - **Matthew 9:13**

6. I will have mercy and not sacrifice. - **Matthew 9:13**

7. For I am not come to call the righteous, but sinners to repentance. - **Matthew 9:13**

8. Can the children of the bridegroom mourn, as long as the bridegroom is with them? - **Matthew 9:15**

9. But the days will come, when the bridegroom shall be taken from them. - **Matthew 9:15**

10. And then shall they fast. - **Matthew 9:15**

September 9

JESUS SAID:

1. No man putteth a piece of new cloth unto an old garment.
   - **Matthew 9:16**

2. For that which is put in to fill it up taketh from the garment.
   - **Matthew 9:16**

3. And the rent is worse. - **Matthew 9:16**

4. Neither do men put new wine into old bottles. - **Matthew 9:17**

5. Else the bottles break and the wine runneth out
   - **Matthew 9:17**

6. And the bottles perish. - **Matthew 9:17**

7. But they put new wine into new bottles. - **Matthew 9:17**

8. And both are preserved. - **Matthew 9:17**

9. Daughter, be of good comfort. - **Matthew 9:22**

10. Thy faith hath made thee whole. - **Matthew 9:22**

September 10
JESUS SAID:

1. Give place, for the maid is not dead, but sleepeth.
   - **Matthew 9:24**

2. Believe ye that I am able to do this? - **Matthew 9:28**

3. According to your faith be it unto you. - **Matthew 9:29**

4. Thy faith hath saved thee; go in peace. - **Luke 7:50**

5. See that no man knows it. - **Matthew 9:30**

6. The harvest truly is plenteous. - **Matthew 9:37**

7. But the labourers are few. - **Matthew 9:37**

8. Pray ye therefore the Lord of the harvest, that He will send labourers into His harvest. - **Matthew 9:37**

9. Go not into the way of the Gentiles. - **Matthew 10:5**

10. And into any city of the Samaritans enter ye not.
    - **Matthew 10:5**

September 11

JESUS SAID:

1. Heal the sick. - **Matthew 10:8**

2. Cleanse the leper. - **Matthew 10:8**

3. Raise the dead. - **Matthew 10:8**

4. Cast out devils. - **Matthew 10:8**

5. Freely ye have received. - **Matthew 10:8**

6. Freely give. - **Matthew 10:8**

7. Provide neither gold, nor silver, nor brass for your purse. - **Matthew 10:9**

8. Nor scrip for your journey, neither two coats, neither shoes, nor yet scarves. - **Matthew 10:10**

9. For the workman is worthy of his meat. - **Matthew 10:10**

10. And into whatsoever city or town ye enter, inquire who in it is worthy; and there abide till ye go thence. - **Matthew 10:11**

September 12

JESUS SAID:

1. The harvest truly is great, but the labourers are few.
   - Luke 10:2

2. Pray ye therefore the Lord of the harvest. **- Luke 10:2**

3. That He would send forth labourers into his harvest.
   - Luke 10:2; Matthew 9:37-38

4. Go your ways; behold I send you forth as lambs (sheep) among wolves. -Luke10;3, **Matthew 10:16**

5. Be ye therefore wise as serpents, and harmless as doves.
   - Matthew 10:16

6. Carry neither purse, nor scrip, nor shoes. and salute no man by the way. **- Luke 10:4**

7. And when ye come into a house, salute it. **- Matthew 10:12**

8. And into whatsoever house ye enter; first say, Peace be to this house. **- Luke 10:5;**

9. And if the house be worth, let your peace come upon it.
   - Matthew 10:13

10. If the son of peace be there your peace shall rest upon it, if not, it shall turn to you again. **- Luke 10:6**

September 13

JESUS SAID:

1. But if the house is not worthy of your peace, let your peace return to you again. - **Matthew 10:13**.

2. And whosoever shall not receive you, nor hear your words. - **Matthew 10:14**

3. When ye depart out of that house or city, shake off the dust of your feet. - **Matthew 10:14**

4. If the son of peace be there, in the same house remain, eating and drinking such things as they give. - **Luke 10:7**

5. For the labourer is worthy of his hire. - **Luke 10:7**

6. Go not from house to house. - **Luke 10:7**

7. And unto whatsoever city ye enter, and they receive you, eat such things as are set before you. - **Luke 10:8**

8. And heal the sick that are therein. - **Luke 10:9**

9. And say unto them. - **Luke 10:9**

10. The kingdom of God is come nigh unto you. - **Luke 10:9**

September 14

JESUS SAID:

1. But into whatsoever city ye enter and they receive you not, go your ways out into the street of the same. - **Luke 10:10**

2. Say, even the very dust of your city, which cleaveth on us, we do wipe off against you. - **Luke 10:10**

3. Say notwithstanding be ye sure of this, that the kingdom of God is come nigh to you. - **Luke 10:11**

4. Verily I say unto you, it shall be more tolerable for the land of Sodom and Gomorrah in the day of judgment, than for that city. - **Matthew 10:15; Luke 10:12; Mark 6:11**

5. Woe unto thee Chorazin. - **Luke 10:13**

6. Woe unto thee Bethsaida. - **Luke 10:13**

7. For if the mighty works had been done in Tyre and Sidon, which have been done in you, they had a great while ago repented. - **Luke 10:13**

8. Sitting in sackcloth and ashes. - **Luke 10:13**

9. But it shall be more tolerable for Tyre and Sidon at the judgement, than for you. - **Luke 10:14**

10. And thou, Capernaum, which are exalted to Heaven, shalt be thrust down to hell. - **Luke 10:15**

September 15

JESUS SAID:

1. He that heareth you heareth me; and he that despiseth you despiseth Me. - **Luke 10:16**

2. And he that despiseth Me despiseth him that sent Me. - **Luke 10:16**

3. Verily, verily, I say unto you, he that receiveth whomsoever I send receiveth Me. - **John 13:20**

4. And he that receiveth Me, receiveth him that sent Me. - **John 13:20**

5. That all men should honour, the Son, even as they honor the Father. - **John 5:23**

6. He that honoureth not the Son, honoureth not the Father which hath sent him. - **John 5:23**

7. Verily, verily, I say unto you, he that heareth My word, and believe on him that sent Me hath everlasting life. - **John 5:24**

8. And they shall not come into condemnation; but is passed from death unto life. - **John 5:24**

9. Verily, verily I say unto you, the hour is coming, and now is when the dead shall hear the voice of the Son of God. - **John 5:25**

10. And they shall hear and live. - **John 5:25**

September 16

JESUS SAID:

1. For as the Father hath life in himself, so hath he given to the Son to have life in himself. - **John 5:26**

2. And hath given him authority to execute judgement also. - **John 5:27**

3. Because he is the Son of man. - **John 5:27**

4. Marvel not at this, for the hour is coming, in the which all that are in the graves shall hear his voice, and come forth; they that have done good, unto the resurrection of life; and they that have done evil, unto the resurrection of damnation. - **John 5:28**

5. I beheld Satan as lightning fall from Heaven. - **Luke 10:18**

6. Behold, I give you power to tread on serpents and scorpions, and over all the power of the enemy. - **Luke 10:19**

7. And nothing shall by any means hurt you. - **Luke 10:19**

8. Notwithstanding in this rejoice not, that the spirits are subject into you. - **Luke 10:20**

9. But rather rejoice, because your names are written in Heaven. - **Luke 10:20**

10. I thank thee, O' Father, Lord of Heaven and earth. - **Luke 10:21**

September 17

JESUS SAID:

1. That thou hast hid these things from the wise and prudent.
   - **Luke 10:21**

2. And thou hast revealed them unto babes. - **Luke 10:21**

3. Even so, Father; for it seem good in Thy sight.
   - **Luke 10:21**; **Matthew 11:26**

4. All things are delivered unto Me of my Father.
   - **Matthew 11:27**; **Luke 10:22**

5. And no man knoweth the Son, but the Father. - **Matthew 11:27**

6. And no man knoweth who the Son is, but the Father.
   - **Luke 10:22**

7. And who the Father is, but the Son and he to whom the Son will reveal him. - **Luke 10:22**

8. Neither, knoweth any man the Father, save the Son and he to whomsoever the Son will reveal. - **Matthew 11:27**

9. Come to Me, all ye that labor and are heavy laden, and I will give you rest. - **Matthew 11:28**

10. Take my yoke upon you, and learn of Me. - **Matthew 11:29**

September 18

JESUS SAID:

1. Take my yoke upon you, and learn of me, for I am meek, and lowly in heart. - **Matthew 11:29**

2. And ye shall find rest unto your souls. - **Matthew 11:29**

3. For My yoke is easy, and My burden is light. - **Matthew 11:30**

4. Blessed are the eyes which see the things that ye see. - **Luke 10:23**

5. For I tell you, that many prophets and kings have desired to see those things which you see, and have not seen them. - **Luke 10:24**

6. And to hear those things which ye hear and have not heard them. - **Luke 10:24; Matthew 13:17**

7. Because it is given unto you to know the mysteries of the kingdom of Heaven. - **Matthew 13:11**

8. But to them it is not given. - **Matthew 13:11**

9. For whosoever hath to him shall be given, and he shall have more abundance. - **Matthew 13:12**

10. But whosoever hath not, from him shall be taken away even that he hath. - **Matthew 13:12**

September 19

JESUS SAID:

1. *Therefore, speak I to them in parables.* - **Matthew 13:13**

2. *Because they seeing see not.* - **Matthew 13:13**

3. *And hearing they hear not.* - **Matthew 13:13**

4. *Neither do they understand.* - **Matthew 13:13**

5. *And in them is fulfilled the prophecy of E-sai-as.*
   - **Matthew 13:14**

6. *Which saith, by hearing ye shall hear, and shall not understand, and by seeing ye shall see; and shall not perceive.*
   - **Matthew 13:14**

7. *For this people's heart is waxed gross and their ears are dull of hearing.* - **Matthew 13:15**

8. *And their eyes have closed.* - **Matthew 13:15**

9. *Lest at any time they should see with their eyes, and hear with their ears.* - **Matthew 13:15**

10. *And they should understand with their hearts, and should be converted, and I should heal them.* - **Matthew 13:15**

September 20

JESUS SAID:

1. Hear ye therefore the parable of the sower. - **Matthew 13:18**
2. When any one heareth the word of the kingdom, and understandeth it not, then comes the wicked one, and catcheth away that which was sown in his heart.
   - **Matthew 13:19**
3. This is he which received seed by the wayside.
   - **Matthew 13:19**
4. But he that received the seed into stony places, the same is he that heareth the word and anon with joy receiveth it.
   - **Matthew 13:20**
5. Yet hath he not a root in himself, but dureth for a while.
   - **Matthew 13:21**
6. For when tribulation or persecution ariseth because of the word, by and by he is offended. - **Matthew 13:21**
7. He also that received seed among the thorns is he that heareth the word; and the cares of this world, and the deceitfulness of riches, choke the word, and be becomes unfruitful. - **Matthew 13:22**
8. But he that received seed into the good ground is he that heareth the word, and understand it. - **Matthew 13:23**
9. Which also beareth fruit. - **Matthew 13:23**
10. And bringeth forth some a hundredfold, some sixty, some thirty. - **Matthew 13:23**

September 21

JESUS SAID:

1. The kingdom of Heaven is likened unto a man which sowed good seed in his field. - **Matthew 13:24**

2. But while men slept, his enemy came and sowed tares among the wheat, and went his way. - **Matthew 13:25**

3. But when the blade was sprung up, and brought forth fruit, then appeared the tares also. - **Matthew 13:26**

4. So the servants of the household came and said unto him, sir, didst not thou sow good seed in thy field? Whence then hath it tares? - **Matthew 13:27**

5. He said unto them, an enemy hath done this. - **Matthew 13:28**

6. The servants said unto him, wilt thou then that we go and gather them up? - **Matthew 13:28**

7. But he said, nay; lest while ye gather up the tares, ye root up the wheat with them. - **Matthew 13:29**

8. Let both grow together until the harvest, and in the time of the harvest, I will say to the reapers. - **Matthew 13:30**

9. Gather ye together first the tares and bind them in bundles to burn them. - **Matthew 13:30**

10. But gather the wheat into my barn. - **Matthew 13:30**

September 22

JESUS SAID:

1. The kingdom of Heaven is like to a mustard seed, which a man took and sowed in his field. - **Matthew 13:31**

2. Which indeed is the least of all seeds, but when it is grown, it is the greatest among herbs, and becometh a tree, so that the birds of the air come and lodge in the branches thereof. - **Matthew 13:32**

3. The kingdom of Heaven is like unto leaven, which a woman took, and hid in three measure of meal, till the whole was leaven. - **Matthew 13:33**

4. He that soweth the good seed is the Son of man. - **Matthew 13:37**

5. The field is the world. - **Matthew 13:38**

6. The good seed are the children of the kingdom. - **Matthew 13:38**

7. But the tares are children of the wicked one. - **Matthew 13:38**

8. The enemy, that sowed them is the devil. - **Matthew 13:39**

9. The harvest is the end of the world. - **Matthew 13:39**

10. And the reapers are the angels. - **Matthew 13:39**

September 23

JESUS SAID:

1. As therefore the tares are gathered and burned in the fire.
   - **Matthew 13:40**

2. So shall it be in the end of this world. - **Matthew 13:40**

3. And the Son of man shall send forth his angels, and they shall gather out of his kingdom all things that offend, and them which do iniquity. - **Matthew 13:41**

4. And shall cast them into a furnace of fire. - **Matthew 13:42**

5. There shall be wailing and gnashing of teeth. - **Matthew 13:42**

6. Then shall the righteous shine forth as the sun in the kingdom of their Father. - **Matthew 13:43**

7. Who hath ears to hear, let him hear. - **Matthew 13:43**

8. Again the kingdom of Heaven is like unto treasure hid in a field. - **Matthew 13:44**

9. The which when a man hath found, he hideth.
   - **Matthew 13:44**

10. And for joy therefore goeth and selleth all that he hath and buyeth that field. - **Matthew 13:44**

September 24

JESUS SAID:

1. Again, the kingdom of Heaven is like unto a merchant man seeking goodly pearls. - **Matthew 13:45**

2. Who when he found one pearl of great price, went and sold all he had, and bought it. - **Matthew 13:46**

3. Again the kingdom of Heaven is like a net, that was cast into the sea and gathered of every kind. - **Matthew 13:47**

4. Which when it was full, they drew to shore, and sat down and gathered the good into vessels, but cast the bad away. - **Matthew 13:48**

5. So shall it be at the end of the world. - **Matthew 13:49**

6. The angels shall come forth and sever the wicked from among the just. - **Matthew 13:49**

7. And shall cast them into the furnace of fire. - **Matthew 13:50**

8. There shall be wailing and gnashing of teeth. - **Matthew 13:50**

9. Have ye understood all these things? - **Matthew 13:51**

10. Therefore every scribe which is instructed unto the kingdom of Heaven is like unto a man that is an householder, which bringeth forth out of his treasure things new and old. - **Matthew 13:52**

September 25

JESUS SAID:

1. They need not depart; give ye them to eat. - **Matthew 14:16**

2. Bring them hither to me. - **Matthew 14:18**

3. Be of good cheer, it is I, be not afraid . - **Matthew 14:27**

4. Come. - **Matthew 14:29**

5. O thou of little faith, wherefore didst thou doubt ?. - **Matthew 14:31**

6. Why do you also transgress the commandments of God by your tradition? - **Matthew 15:3**

7. For God commanded, saying honor thy father and mother. - **Matthew 15:4**

8. He that curseth his father or mother, let him die the death. - **Matthew 15:4**

9. But ye say, whosoever shall say to his father or his mother, it is a gift, by whatsoever thou mightest be profited by me. - **Matthew 15:5**

10. And honor not his father or his mother, he shall be free, thus have ye made the commandment of God of none effect by your tradition. - **Matthew 15:6**

September 26

JESUS SAID:

1. Ye hypocrites, well did Esaias prophesy of you saying, this people draw nigh unto me with their mouth, and honoureth me with their lips, but their hearts is far from me.
   - **Matthew 15:7-8; Mark 7:6**

2. But in vain they do worship me, teaching for doctrines the commandments of men. - **Matthew 15:9**

3. Hear and understand. - **Matthew 15:10**

4. For laying aside the commandments of God; ye hold the traditions of men as the washing of pots and cups. - **Mark 7:8**

5. And many other such like things ye do. - **Mark 7:8**

6. Full well ye reject the commandment of God, that ye may keep your own tradition. - **Mark 7:9**

7. For Moses said, honor thy father and thy mother. - **Mark 7:10**

8. Moses said, who so curseth father or mother let him die the death. - **Mark 7:10**

9. But ye say, if a man shall say to his father or mother, it is a corban (that is to say, a gift), by whatsoever thou mightest be profited by me, he shall be free. - **Mark 7:11**

10. And ye suffer him no more to do aught for his father or his mother. - **Mark 7:12**

September 27

JESUS SAID:

1. Making the word of God of none effect through your traditions, which ye have delivered, and the many such like things do ye. - **Mark 7:13**

2. Hearken unto me every one of you and understand, there is nothing from without a man, that entering into him can defile him. - **Mark 7:14**-15

3. But the things which come out of him, those are they that defile the man. - **Mark 7:15**

4. Every plant, which my Heavenly Father hath not planted, shall be rooted up. - **Matthew 15:13**

5. If any man have ears to hear, let him hear. - **Mark 7:16**

6. Let them alone, they be blind leaders of the blind. - **Matthew 15:14**

7. And if the blind lead the blind, both shall fall into the ditch. - **Matthew 15:14**

8. Are ye also without understanding. - **Matthew 15:16**

9. Do you not yet understand that what entereth into the mouth of a man, goeth into the belly, enters not into the heart, and is cast out into the draught? - **Mark 7:18**-19; **Matthew 15:17**

10. But those things which proceed out of the mouth come forth from the heart; and they defile the man. - **Matthew 15:18**

September 28

JESUS SAID:

1. For out of the heart proceed evil thoughts, murders, adulteries, fornications, thefts, false witness, blasphemies. – **Matthew 15:19; Mark 7:21**

2. For from within out of the heart of men proceed, covetousness, wickedness, deceit, lasciviousness, an evil eye, blasphemy, pride, foolishness. – **Mark 7:22**

3. These are the things which defile a man; but to eat with unwashed hands defileth not a man. – **Matthew 15:20**

4. All these evil things come from within, and defile the man. – **Mark 7:23**

5. Let the children first be filled, for it is not meet to take the children's bread and cast it unto the dogs. – **Mark 7:27**

6. I am not sent but unto the lost sheep of the house of Israel. – **Matthew 15:24**

7. For this saying, go thy way. – **Mark 7:29**

8. The devil is gone out of thy daughter. – **Mark 7:29**

9. O woman, great is thy faith; be it unto thee even as thou wilt. – **Matthew 15:28**

10. Ephphatha (be opened). – **Mark 7:34**

September 29

JESUS SAID:

1. I have compassion on the multitude because they have now been with me three days and have nothing to eat.
   - **Mark 8:2**; **Matthew 15:32**

2. And if I send them away fasting to their own houses, they will faint by the way. - **Mark 8:3**; **Matthew 15:32**

3. For divers of them came from far. - **Mark 8:3**

4. How many loaves have ye? - **Mark 8:5**; **Matthew 15:34**

5. O ye of little faith, why reason ye among yourselves, because ye have brought no bread. - **Matthew 16:8**; **Mark 8:17**

6. Perceive ye not yet neither understand? - **Mark 8:17**

7. Have ye your heart yet hardened ? - **Mark 8:17**

8. Do you not yet understand neither remember the five loaves and of the five thousand, and how many baskets ye took up ?
   - **Matthew 16:9**

9. Neither the seven loaves of the four thousand.
   - **Matthew 16:10**

10. And how many baskets ye took up?
    - **Matthew 16:10**; **Mark 8:20**

September 30

JESUS SAID:

1. How is it ye do not understand that I spake it not to you concerning bread. - **Matthew 16:11**

2. That ye should beware of the leaven of the Pharisees and of the Sadducees. - **Matthew 16:11**

3. How is it that ye do not understand? - **Mark 8:21**

4. To the blind man (after restoring his sight), neither go into the town, nor tell it to any in the town. - **Mark 8:26**

5. Who do men say I am ? - **Mark 8:27; Luke 9:18**

6. Whom do men say that I the Son of man am? - **Matthew 16:13**

7. But whom say ye that I am ?
   - **Matthew 16:15; Mark 8:29; Luke 9:20**

8. (When Peter answered him) Blessed art thou Simon Barjona.
   - **Matthew 16:17**

9. For flesh and blood hath not revealed it unto thee, but my Father which is in Heaven. - **Matthew 16:17**

10. And I say also unto thee that thou art Peter, and upon this rock I will build my church, and the gates of hell shall not prevail against it. - **Matthew 16:18**

October 1

JESUS SAID:

1. And I will give unto thee the keys of the kingdom of Heaven. - **Matthew 16:19; Matthew 18:18)**
2. And whatsoever thou shalt bind on earth shall be bound in Heaven. - **Matthew 16:19; Matthew 18:18**
3. And whatsoever thou shalt loose on earth shall be loosed in Heaven. - **Matthew 16:19; Matthew 18:18**
4. If any man will come after me, let him deny himself and take up his cross, and follow me. - **Matthew 16:24**
5. For what is a man profited, if he gain the whole world and lose his own soul? - **Matthew 16:26**
6. Or what shall a man give in exchange for his soul. - **Matthew 16:26**
7. He that loveth his life shall lose it and he that hateth his life in this world shall keep it unto life eternal. - **John 12:25**
8. Verily I say unto you, there be some standing here which will not taste of death, till they see the Son of man coming in his kingdom. - **Matthew 16:28**
9. The hour is come that the Son of man should be glorified. - **John 12:23**
10. Verily, verily, I say unto you, except a corn of wheat fall into the ground and die, it abideth alone; but if it die, it bringeth forth much fruit. - **John 12:24**

October 2

JESUS SAID:

1. Woman believe me, the hour cometh, when ye shall neither in this mountain, not yet a Jerusalem worship the Father. - **John 4:21**

2. Ye worship ye know not what; we know what we worship, for salvation is of the Jews. - **John 4:22**

3. But the hour cometh and now is, when the true worshippers shall worship the Father in spirit and in truth. - **John 4:23**

4. For the Father seeketh such to worship him. - **John 4:23**

5. God is a Spirit. - **John 4:24**

6. And they that worship him must worship him in spirit and in truth. - **John 4:24**

7. I that speak unto thee am he. - **John 4:26**

8. I have meat to eat that ye know not of. - **John 4:32**

9. My meat is to do the will of him that sent me. - **John 4:34**

10. And to finish his work. - **John 4:34**

October 3

JESUS SAID:

1. And he that reapeth receiveth wages, and gather fruit unto life eternal. - **John 4:36**

2. That both he that soweth and he that reapeth may rejoice together. - **John 4:36**

3. And herein is that saying true, one soweth, and another reapeth. - **John 4:37**

4. I sent you to reap that whereon ye bestowed no labor. - **John 4:38**

5. Other men labored and ye entered into their labors. - **John 4:38**

6. I can of mine own self do nothing. - **John 5:30**

7. As I hear, I judge and my judgement is just. - **John 5:30**

8. Because I seek not mine own will. - **John 5:30**

9. But the will of the Father which hath sent me. - **John 5:30**

10. If I bear witness of myself, my witness is not true. - **John 5:31**

October 4

JESUS SAID:

1. There is another that beareth witness of me. - **John 5:32**

2. And I know that the witness which he witnesseth of me is true. - **John 5:32**

3. Ye sent unto John and he bare witness unto the truth. - **John 5:33**

4. But I receive not testimony from man. - **John 5:34**

5. But these things I say, that ye might be saved. - **John 5:34**

6. He was a burning and shining light and ye were willing for a season to rejoice in his light. - **John 5:35**

7. But I have a greater witness than that of John. - **John 5:36**

8. For the works which the Father hath given me to finish the same works that I do, bear witness of me, that the Father hath sent me. - **John 5:36**

9. And the Father himself which hath sent me, hath borne witness of me. - **John 5:37**

10. Ye have neither heard his voice at any time, nor seen his shape and ye have not his word abiding in you: for whom he has sent, him ye believe not. - **John 5:37-38**

October 5

JESUS SAID:

1. Search the scriptures, for in them ye think ye have eternal life. - **John 5:39**

2. And they are they which testify of me. - **John 5:39**

3. And ye will not come to me that ye might have life. - **John 5:40**

4. I receive not honor from men. - **John 5:41**

5. But I know you. - **John 5:42**

6. That ye have not the love of God in you. - **John 5:42**

7. I am come in my Father's name, and ye receive me not. - **John 5:43**

8. If another shall come in his own name, him ye will receive. - **John 5:43**

9. How can ye believe which receive honor one of another. - **John 5:44**

10. And seek not the honor that cometh from God only? - **John 5:44**

October 6

JESUS SAID:

1. Do not think that I will accuse you to the Father. – **John 5:45**

2. There is one that accuseth you, even Moses, in whom ye trust . – **John 5:45**

3. For had ye believed Moses, you would have believed me, for he wrote of me. – **John 5:46**

4. But if ye believe not his writings, how shall ye believe my words? – **John 5:47**

5. Verily, verily, I say unto you, ye seek me, not because ye saw the miracles, but because ye did eat of the loaves and were filled. – **John 6:26**

6. Labor not for the meat which perisheth. – **John 6:27**

7. But for that meat which endureth unto everlasting life. – **John 6:27**

8. Which the Son of man shall give unto you for him hath God the Father sealed .– **John 6:27**

9. This is the work of God. – **John 6:29**

10. That ye believe on him whom he hath sent. – **John 6:29**

October 7

JESUS SAID:

1. Verily, verily I say unto you, Moses gave you not that bread from Heaven. - **John 6:32**

2. But my Father giveth you the true bread from Heaven. - **John 6:32**

3. For the bread of God is he that cometh down from Heaven and giveth life unto the world. - **John 6:33**

4. I am the bread of life. - **John 6:35**

5. He that cometh to me shall never hunger. - **John 6:35**

6. He that believeth on me shall never thirst. - **John 6:35**

7. But I said unto you, that ye also have seen me and believe not. - **John 6:36**

8. All that the Father giveth me shall come to me. - **John 6:37**

9. And him that cometh to me, I will in no wise cast out. - **John 6:37**

10. For I came down from Heaven, not to do mine own will, but the will of him that sent me. - **John 6:38**

October 8

JESUS SAID:

1. And this is the Father's will which hath sent me. - **John 6:39**

2. That of all which he hath given me I should lose nothing. - **John 6:39**

3. But should raise it up again at the last day. - **John 6:39**

4. And this is the will of him that sent me. - **John 6:40**

5. That everyone which seeth the Son, and believeth on him, may have everlasting life. - **John 6:40**

6. And I will raise him up at the last day. - **John 6:40**

7. I am the bread which came down from Heaven. - **John 6:41**

8. I came down from Heaven ? - **John 6:42**

9. Murmur not among yourselves. - **John 6:43**

10. No man can come to me, except the Father which hath sent me draw him; and I will raise him up at the last day. - **John 6:44**

October 9

JESUS SAID:

1. It is written in the prophets, and they shall be all taught of God. - **John 6:45**

2. Every man therefore that hath heard, and hath learned of the Father, cometh unto me. - **John 6:45**

3. Not that any man hath seen the Father, save he which is of God. - **John 6:46**

4. He hath seen the Father. - **John 6:46**

5. Verily, verily, I say unto you, he that believeth on me hath everlasting life. - **John 6:47**

6. I am that bread of life. - **John 6:48**

7. Your fathers did eat manna in the wilderness, and are dead. - **John 6:49**

8. This is the bread which cometh down from Heaven. - **John 6:50**

9. That a man may eat thereof, and not die. - **John 6:50**

10. I am the living bread which came down from Heaven. - **John 6:51**

October 10

JESUS SAID:

1. *If any man eat of this bread, he shall live forever.* - **John 6:51**

2. *And the bread that I will give is my flesh, which I will give for the life of the world.* - **John 6:51**

3. *Verily, verily, I say unto you, except ye eat the flesh of the Son of man, and drink his blood, ye have no life in you.* - **John 6:53**

4. *Whoso eateth my flesh and drinketh my blood, hath eternal life.* - **John 6:54**

5. *And I will raise him up at the last day.* - **John 6:54**

6. *For my flesh is meat indeed, and my blood is drink indeed.* - **John 6:55**

7. *He that eateth my flesh and drinketh my blood, dwelleth in me, and I in him.* - **John 6:56**

8. *As the living Father hath sent me, and I live by the Father.* - **John 6:57**

9. *So he that eateth me, even he shall live by me.* - **John 6:57**

10. *This is the bread that came down from Heaven, not as your fathers did eat manna, and are dead, he that eateth of this bread shall live forever.* - **John 6:58**

October 11

JESUS SAID:

1. Doth this offend you. - **John 6:61**

2. What and if ye shall see the Son of man ascend up where he was before. - **John 6:62**

3. It is the spirit that quickeneth. - **John 6:63**

4. The flesh profiteth nothing. - **John 6:63**

5. The words that I speak unto you, they are spirit, and they are life. - **John 6:63**

6. But there are some of you that believe not. - **John 6:64**

7. Therefore, said I unto you, that no man can come unto me, except it were given unto him of my Father. - **John 6:65**

8. Will ye also go away? - **John 6:67**

9. Have not I chosen you twelve, and one of you is a devil? - **John 6:70**

10. My time is not yet come: but your time is always ready. - **John 7:6**

October 12

JESUS SAID:

1. The world cannot hate you; but me it hateth, because I testify of it, that the works thereof are evil. – **John 7:7**

2. Go ye up unto this feast, I go not up unto this feast, for my time is not yet full come. – **John 7:8**

3. My doctrine is not mine, but his that sent me. – **John 7:16**

4. If any man will do his will, he shall know of the doctrine, whether it be of God, or whether I speak of myself. – **John 7:17**

5. He that speaketh of himself seeketh his own glory. – **John 7:18**

6. But he that seeketh his glory that sent him, the same is true and no unrighteousness is in him. – **John 7:18**

7. Did not Moses give you the law, and yet none of you keepeth the law? – **John 7:19**

8. Why go ye about to kill me? – **John 7:19**

9. I have done one work, and ye all marvel. – **John 7:21**

10. Moses therefore gave unto you circumcision (not because it is of Moses, but of the Father's) and ye on the Sabbath day circumcise a man. – **John 7:22**

October 13

JESUS SAID:

1. If a man on the Sabbath day receive circumcision, that the law of Moses should not be broken, are ye angry at me, because I have made a man every whit whole on the Sabbath day? - **John 7:23**

2. Judge not according to the appearance, but judge righteous judgement. - **John 7:24**

3. Ye both know me and ye know whence I am. - **John 7:28**

4. And I am not come of myself, but he that sent me is true, whom ye know not. - **John 7:28**

5. But I know him for I am from him, and he hath sent me. - **John 7:29**

6. Yet a little while I am with you, and then I go unto him that sent me. - **John 7:33**

7. Ye shall seek me and shall not find me. - **John 7:34**

8. And where I am thither ye cannot come. - **John 7:34**

9. If any man thirst, let him come unto me and drink. - **John 7:37**

10. He that believeth on me, as the scripture hath said, out of his belly shall flow rivers of living water. - **John 7:38**

October 14

JESUS SAID:

1. He that is without sin among you, let him first cast a stone at her. - **John 8:7**

2. Woman where are those thine accusers? - **John 8:10**

3. Hath no man condemned thee? - **John 8:10**

4. Neither do I condemn thee. - **John 8:11**

5. Go and sin no more. - **John 8:11**

6. I am the light of the world. - **John 8:12**

7. He that followeth me shall not walk in darkness. - **John 8:12**

8. But shall have the light of life. - **John 8:12**

9. Though I bear record of myself, yet my record is true. - **John 8:14**

10. For I know whence I came, and whither I go, but ye cannot tell whence I come, and whither I go. - **John 8:14**

October 15

JESUS SAID:

1. Ye judge after the flesh. - **John 8:15**

2. I judge no man. - **John 8:15**

3. And yet if I judge my judgement is true. - **John 8:16**

4. For I am not alone. - **John 8:16**

5. For I am not alone, but I and the Father that sent me. - **John 8:16**

6. It is also written in your law, that the testimony of two men is true. - **John 8:17**

7. I am one that bear witness of myself. - **John 8:18**

8. And the Father that sent me beareth witness of me. - **John 8:18**

9. Ye neither know me, nor my Father. - **John 8:19**

10. If ye had known me, ye should have known my Father also. - **John 8:19**

October 16

JESUS SAID:

1. *I go my way and ye shall seek me, and ye shall die in your sins.* - **John 8:21**

2. *Whither I go ye cannot come.* - **John 8:21-22**

3. *Ye are from beneath.* - **John 8:23**

4. *I am from above.* - **John 8:23**

5. *Ye are of this world.* - **John 8:23**

6. *I am not of this world.* - **John 8:23**

7. *I said therefore unto you, that ye shall die in your sins.* - **John 8:24**

8. *For if ye believe not that I am he, ye shall die in your sins.* - **John 8:24**

9. *Even the same that I said, unto you from the beginning.* - **John 8:25**

10. *I have many things to say and to judge of you, but he that sent me is true, and I speak to the world those things which I have heard of him.* - **John 8:26**

October 17

JESUS SAID:

1. When ye have lifted up the Son of man, then shall ye know that I am he. - **John 8:28**

2. And that I do nothing of myself, but as my Father hath taught me. - **John 8:28**

3. I speak these things. - **John 8:28**

4. And he that sent me is with me. - **John 8:29**

5. The Father hath not left me alone. - **John 8:29**

6. For I do always those things that please him. - **John 8:29**

7. If ye continue in my word, then ye are my disciples indeed. - **John 8:31**

8. And ye shall know the truth, and the truth shall make you free. - **John 8:32**

9. Ye shall be made free. - **John 8:33**

10. Verily, verily I say unto you, whosoever committeth sin is the servant of sin. - **John 8:34**

October 18

JESUS SAID:

1. And the servant abideth not in the house forever, but the Son abideth ever. - **John 8:35**

2. If the Son therefore shall make you free, ye shall be free indeed. - **John 8:36**

3. I know that ye are Abraham's seed. - **John 8:37**

4. But ye seek to kill me. - **John 8:37**

5. Because my word hath no place in you. - **John 8:37**

6. I speak that which I have seen with my Father. - **John 8:38**

7. And ye do that which ye have seen with your father. - **John 8:38**

8. If ye were Abraham's children, ye would do the works of Abraham. - **John 8:39**

9. But now ye seek to kill me, a man that hath told you the truth, which I have heard from God. - **John 8:40**

10. This did not Abraham. - **John 8:40**

October 19
JESUS SAID:

1. Ye do the deeds of your father. - **John 8:41**

2. If God were your Father, ye would love me. - **John 8:42**

3. For I proceed forth and came from God. - **John 8:42**

4. Neither came I of myself, but he sent me. - **John 8:42**

5. Why do ye not understand my speech? - **John 8:43**

6. Even because ye cannot hear my word. - **John 8:43**

7. Ye are of your father the devil. - **John 8:44**

8. And the lusts of your father ye will do. - **John 8:44**

9. He was a murderer from the beginning, and abode not in the truth, because there is no truth in him. - **John 8:44**

10. When he speaketh a lie, he speaketh of his own; for he is a liar, and the father of it. - **John 8:44**

October 20

JESUS SAID:

1. And because I tell you the truth, ye believe me not. - **John 8:45**

2. Which of you convinceth me of sin? - **John 8:46**

3. And if I say the truth, why do ye not believe me? - **John 8:46**

4. He that is of God heareth God's words. - **John 8:47**

5. Ye therefore hear them not, because ye are not of God. - **John 8:47**

6. I have not a devil, but I honor my Father, and ye do dishonor me. - **John 8:49**

7. And I seek not mine own glory. - **John 8:50**

8. There is one that seeketh and judgeth. - **John 8:50**

9. Verily, verily, I say unto you, if a man keep my saying, he shall never see death. - **John 8:51**

10. If a man keep my saying, he shall never taste of death. - **John 8:52**

October 21

JESUS SAID:

1. If I honor myself, my honor is nothing. - **John 8:54**

2. It is my Father that honoureth me; of whom you say, that he is your God. - **John 8:54**

3. Yet ye have not known him. - **John 8:55**

4. But I know him. - **John 8:55**

5. And if I should say, I know him not, I shall be a liar like you. - **John 8:55**

6. But I know him and keep his saying. - **John 8:55**

7. Your father Abraham rejoiced to see my day. - **John 8:56**

8. And he saw it and was glad. - **John 8:56**

9. Verily, verily I say unto you, before Abraham was, I am. - **John 8:58**

10. Neither hath this man sinned, nor his parents, but that the works of God should be made manifest in him. - **John 9:3**

October 22

JESUS SAID:

1. *I must work the works of him that sent me, while it is day.* – **John 9:4**

2. *The night cometh when no man can work.* – **John 9:4**

3. *As long as I am in the world, I am the light of the world.* – **John 9:5**

4. *Go, wash in the pool of Siloam.* – **John 9:7**

5. *Go to the pool of Siloam and wash.* – **John 9:11**

6. *Dost thou believe on the Son of God.* – **John 9:35**

7. *Thou hast both seen him, and it is he that talketh with thee.* – **John 9:37**

8. *For judgement I am come into this world.* – **John 9:39**

9. *That they which see not might see.* – **John 9:39**

10. *And they which see might be made blind.* – **John 9:39**

October 23

JESUS SAID:

1. *If ye were blind, ye should have no sin.* - **John 9:41**

2. *But now ye say, we see, therefore your sin remaineth.* - **John 9:41**

3. *Verily, verily, I say into you, he that entereth not by the door unto the sheepfold, but climbeth up some other way, the same is a thief and a robber.* - **John 10:1**

4. *But he that entereth in by the door is the shepherd of the sheep.* - **John 10:2**

5. *To him the porter openeth.* - **John 10:3**

6. *And the sheep heareth his voice.* - **John 10:3**

7. *And he calleth his own sheep by name.* - **John 10:3**

8. *And leadeth them out.* - **John 10:3**

9. *And when he putteth forth his own sheep, he goeth before them.* - **John 10:4**

10. *And the sheep follow him; for they know his voice.* - **John 10:4**

October 24

JESUS SAID:

1. And a stranger will they not follow. - **John 10:5**

2. But will flee from him for they know not the voice of strangers. - **John 10:5**

3. Verily, verily, I say unto you, I am the door of the sheep. - **John 10:7**

4. All that ever came before me are thieves and robbers. - **John 10:8**

5. But the sheep did not hear them. - **John 10:8**

6. I am the door. - **John 10:9**

7. By me if any man enter in, he shall be saved, and shall go in and out, and find pasture. - **John 10:9**

8. The thief cometh not, but to steal, and to kill and to destroy. - **John 10:10**

9. I am come that they might have life. - **John 10:10**

10. And that they might have it more abundantly. - **John 10:10**

October 25

JESUS SAID:

1. I am the good shepherd. – **John 10:11**

2. The good shepherd giveth his life for the sheep. – **John 10:11**

3. But he that is an hireling and not the shepherd, whose own the sheep are not, seeth the wolf coming, and leaveth the sheep and fleeth. – **John 10:12**

4. And the wolf catcheth them, and scattereth the sheep. – **John 10:12**

5. The hireling fleeth because he is a hireling, and careth not for the sheep. – **John 10:13**

6. I am the good shepherd and know my sheep, and am known of mine. – **John 10:14**

7. As the Father knoweth me, even so know I the Father. – **John 10:15**

8. And I lay down my life for the sheep. – **John 10:15**

9. And other sheep, I have which are not of this fold, them also I must bring. – **John 10:16**

10. And they shall hear my voice; and there shall be one fold, and one shepherd. – **John 10:16**

October 26

JESUS SAID:

1. Therefore doth my Father love me, because I lay down my life, that I might take it again. - **John 10:17**

2. No man taketh it from me. - **John 10:18**

3. But I lay it down of myself. - **John 10:18**

4. I have power to lay it down, and I have power to take it again. - **John 10:18**

5. This commandment have I received of my Father. - **John 10:18**

6. I told you, and you believed not. - **John 10:25**

7. The works that I do in my Father's name, they bear witness of me. - **John 10:25**

8. But ye believe not because ye are not of my sheep, as I said unto you. - **John 10:26**

9. My sheep hear my voice. - **John 10:27**

10. And I know them and they follow me. - **John 10:27**

October 27

JESUS SAID:

1. And I give unto them eternal life. - **John 10:28**

2. And they shall never perish. - **John 10:28**

3. Neither shall any man pluck them out of my hand.
   - **John 10:28**

4. My Father, which gave them me, is greater than all.
   - **John 10:29**

5. And no man is able to pluck them out of my Father's hand. - **John 10:29**

6. I and my Father are one. - **John 10:30**

7. Many good works have I shewed you from my Father.
   - **John 10:32**

8. For which of these works do ye stone me. - **John 10:32**

9. Is it not written in your law, I said ye are gods? - **John 10:34**

10. If he called them gods, unto whom the word of God came, and the scripture cannot be broken, say ye of him, whom the Father hath sanctified, and sent into the world. Thou blasphemest; because I said, I am the Son of God ?
    - **John 10:35,36**

October 28

JESUS SAID:

1. *If I do not the works of my Father, believe me not.*
   – **John 10:37**

2. *But if I do though ye believe not me, believe the works.*
   – **John 10:38**

3. *That ye may know and believe, that the Father is in me and I in him.* – **John 10:38**

4. *This sickness is not unto death,* – **John 11-4**

5. *But for the glory of God.* – **John 11:4**

6. *That the Son of God might be glorified thereby.* – **John 11:4**

7. *Let us go into Judaea again.* – **John 11:7**

8. *Are there not twelve hours in the day?* – **John 11:9**

9. *If any man walk in the day, he stumbleth not, because he seeth the light of the world.* – **John 11:9**

10. *But if a man walk in the night, he stumbleth, because there is no light in him.* – **John 11:10**

October 29

JESUS SAID:

1. *Our friend Lazarus sleepeth, but I go, that I may awake him out of sleep.* - **John 11:11**

2. *Lazarus is dead.* - **John 11:14**

3. *And I am glad for your sakes that I was not there to the intent ye may believe.* - **John 11:15**

4. *Nevertheless let us go unto him.* - **John 11:15**

5. *Thy brother shall rise again.* - **John 11:23**

6. *I am the resurrection and the life.* - **John 11:25**

7. *He that believeth in me, though he were dead, yet shall live.* - **John 11:25**

8. *And whosoever liveth and believe in me shall never die.* - **John 11:26**

9. *Believest thou this?* - **John 11:26**

10. *Where have ye laid him?* - **John 11:34**

October 30

JESUS SAID:

1. Take ye away the stone. – **John 11:39**

2. Said I not unto thee, that, if thou wouldest believe, thou shouldest see the glory of God? – **John 11:40**

3. Father, I thank thee that thou hast heard me. – **John 11:41**

4. And I knew that thou hearest me always. – **John 11:42**

5. But because of the people which stand by I said it. – **John 11:42**

6. That they may believe that thou hast sent me. – **John 11:42**

7. Lazarus, come forth. – **John 11:43**

8. Loose him, and let him go. – **John 11:44**

9. Let her alone: against the day of my burying hath she kept this. – **John 12:7**

10. For the poor always ye have with you, but me ye have not always. – **John 12:8**

October 31

JESUS SAID:

1. The hour is come that the Son of man should be glorified. - **John 12:23**

2. Verily, verily I say unto you, except a corn of wheat fall to the ground and die, it abideth alone. - **John 12:24**

3. But if it die, it bringeth forth much fruit. - **John 12:24**

4. He that loveth his life shall lose it. - **John 12:25**

5. And he that hateth his life in the world shall keep it unto life eternal. - **John 12:25**

6. If any man serve me, let him follow me. - **John 12:26**

7. And where I am, there shall also my servants be. - **John 12:26**

8. If any man serve me, him will my Father honor. - **John 12:26**

9. Now is my soul troubled, and what shall I say? - **John 12:27**

10. Father, save me from this hour : but for this cause came I unto this hour. - **John 12:27**

November 1

JESUS SAID:

1. Father glorify thy name. - **John 12:28**

2. This voice came not because of me, but for your sakes. - **John 12:30**

3. Now is the judgment of this world. - **John 12:31**

4. Now shall the prince of the world be cast out. - **John 12:31**

5. And I, if I be lifted up from the earth, will draw all men unto me. - **John 12:32**

6. The Son of man must be lifted up? - **John 12:34**

7. Yet a little while is the light with you. - **John 12:35**

8. Walk while ye have light, lest darkness comes upon you. - **John 12:35**

9. For he that walketh in darkness knoweth not whither he goeth. - **John 12:35**

10. While ye have light, believe in the light, that ye may be the children of light. - **John 12:36**

November 2

JESUS SAID:

1. He that believeth on me, believeth not on me, but on him that sent me. - **John 12:44**

2. And he that seeth me seeth him that sent me. - **John 12:45**

3. I am come a light into the world. - **John 12:46**

4. That whosoever believeth on me shall not abide in darkness. - **John 12:46**

5. And if any man hear my words, and believe not, I judge him not. - **John 12:47**

6. For I came not to judge the world, but to save the world. - **John 12:47**

7. He that rejecteth me, and receiveth not my words, hath one that judgeth him. - **John 12:48**

8. The word that I have spoken, the same shall judge him in the last day. - **John 12:48**

9. For I have not spoken of myself, but the Father which sent me, he gave me a commandment, what I should say, and what I should speak - **John 12:49**

10. And I know that his commandment is life everlasting: whatsoever I speak therefore, even as the Father said unto me, so I speak. - **John 12:50**

November 3

JESUS SAID:

1. What I do, thou knowest not now, but thou shalt know hereafter. - **John 13:7**

2. If I wash thee not, thou hast no part with me. - **John 13:8**

3. He that is washed needeth not save to wash his feet, but is clean every whit. - **John 13:10**

4. And ye are clean, but not all. - **John 13:10**

5. Ye are not all clean. - **John 13:11**

6. Know ye what I have done to you? - **John 13:12**

7. Ye call me Master and Lord and ye say well, for so I am. - **John 13:13**

8. If I then, your Lord and Master, have washed your feet; ye also ought to wash one another's feet. - **John 13:14**

9. For I have given you an example, that ye should do as I have done to you. - **John 13:15**

10. Verily, verily, I say unto you, the servant is not greater than his lord, neither he that is sent greater than he that sent him. - **John 13:16**

November 4

JESUS SAID:

1. *If you know these things, happy are ye if ye do them.*
   – John 13:17

2. *I speak not of you all, I know whom I have chosen.*
   – John 13:18

3. *But that the scripture may be fulfilled.* **– John 13:18**

4. *He that eateth bread with me hath lifted up his heel against me.* **– John 13:18**

5. *Now I tell you before it come, that, when it is come to pass, ye may believe that I am he.* **– John 13:19**

6. *Verily, verily, I say unto you, he that receiveth whomsoever I send receiveth me.* **– John 13:20**

7. *And he that receiveth me receiveth him that sent me.*
   – John 13:20

8. *Verily, verily, I say unto you, that one of you shall betray me.*
   – John 13:21

9. *He it is to whom I shall give a sop, when I have dipped it.*
   – John 13:26

10. *That thou doest, do it quickly.* **– John 13:27**

November 5
JESUS SAID:

1. Now is the Son of man glorified. - **John 13:31**
2. And God is glorified in him. - **John 13:31**
3. If God be glorified in him, God shall also glorify him in himself, and shall straightway glorify him. - **John 13:32**
4. Little children yet a little while I am with you. - **John 13:33**
5. Ye shall seek me. - **John 13:33**
6. And as I said unto the Jews, whither I go, ye cannot come. - **John 13:33**
7. So now I say to you. - **John 13:33**
8. A new commandment I give unto you. - **John 13:34**
9. That ye love one another; as I have loved you, that ye also love one another. - **John 13:34**
10. By this shall all men know that ye are my disciples, if ye have love one to another. **John 13:35**

November 6

JESUS SAID:

1. Whither I go, thou canst not follow me now, but thou shalt follow me afterwards. - **John 13:36**

2. Wilt thou lay down thy life for my sake? - **John 13:38**

3. Verily, verily I say unto thee, the cock shall not crow, till thou hast denied me thrice. - **John 13:38**

4. Let not your heart be troubled. - **John 14:1**

5. Ye believe in God, believe also in me. - **John 14:1**

6. In my Father's house are many mansions. - **John 14:2**

7. If it were not so I would have told you. - **John 14:2**

8. I go to prepare a place for you. - **John 14:2**

9. And if I go and prepare a place for you, I will come again, and receive you unto myself, that where I am, there ye may be also. - **John 14:3**

10. And whither I go ye know, and the way ye know. - **John 14:4**

November 7

JESUS SAID:

1. I am the way, the truth, and the life. - **John 14:6**

2. No man cometh unto the Father, but by me. - **John 14:6**

3. If ye had known me, ye should have known my Father also. - **John 14:7**

4. And from henceforth ye know him, and have seen him. - **John 14:7**

5. Have I been so long time with you, and yet hast thou not known me Philip? - **John 14:9**

6. He that hath seen me hath seen the Father. - **John 14:9**

7. And how sayest thou then, shew us the Father? - **John 14:9**

8. Believest thou not that I am in the Father and the Father is in me? - **John 14:10**

9. The words that I speak unto you I speak not of myself. - **John 14:10**

10. I speak not myself, but the Father that dwelleth in me, he doeth the works. - **John 14:10**

November 8

JESUS SAID:

1. Believe me that I am in the Father and the Father in me. - **John 14:11**

2. Or else believe me for the very works' sake. - **John 14:11**

3. Verily, verily, I say unto you, he that believeth on me, the works that I do shall he do also. - **John 14:12**

4. And greater works than these shall he do. - **John 14:12**

5. Because I go unto my Father. - **John 14:12**

6. And whatsoever ye shall ask in my name, that will I do. - **John 14:13**

7. That the Father may be glorified in the Son. - **John 14:13**

8. If ye ask anything in my name, I will do it. - **John 14:14**

9. If you love me, keep my commandments. - **John 14:15**

10. And I will pray the Father and he shall give you another Comforter, that he may abide with you forever. - **John 14:16**

November 9

JESUS SAID:

1. Even the Spirit of truth; whom the world cannot receive because, it seeth him not. – **John 14:17**

2. Neither knoweth him. – **John 14:17**

3. But ye know him. – **John 14:17**

4. For he dwelleth with you. – **John 14:17**

5. And shall be in you. – **John 14:17**

6. I will not leave you comfortless. – **John 14:18**

7. I will come to you. – **John 14:18**

8. Yet a little while, and the world seeth me no more. – **John 14:19**

9. But ye see me. – **John 14:19**

10. Because I live, ye shall live also. – **John 14:19**

November 10

JESUS SAID:

1. At that day ye shall know that I am in my Father, and ye in me, and I in you. - **John 14:20**

2. He that hath my commandments, and keepeth them, he it is that loveth me. - **John 14:21**

3. And he that loveth me shall be loved of my Father. - **John 14:21**

4. And I will love him, and will manifest myself to him. - **John 14:21**

5. If a man love me, he will keep my words. - **John 14:23**

6. And my Father will love him. - **John 14:23**

7. And we will come unto him. - **John 14:23**

8. And make our abode with him. - **John 14:23**

9. He that loveth me not keepeth not my sayings. - **John 14:24**

10. And the word which ye hear is not mine, but the Father's which sent me. - **John 14:24**

November 11

JESUS SAID:

1. These things have I spoken unto you, being yet present with you. - **John 14:25**

2. But the Comforter which is the Holy Ghost, whom the Father will send in my name, he shall teach you all things. - **John 14:26**

3. And bring all things to your remembrance, whatsoever I have said unto you. - **John 14:26**

4. Peace I leave with you. - **John 14:27**

5. My peace I give unto you. - **John 14:27**

6. Not as the world giveth. - **John 14:27**

7. Give I unto you. - **John 14:27**

8. Let not your heart be troubled. - **John 14:27**

9. Neither let it be afraid. - **John 14:27**

10. Ye have heard how I said unto you, I go away, and come again unto you. – **John 14:28**

November 12

JESUS SAID:

1. *If ye loved me, ye would rejoice.* - **John 14:28**

2. *Because I said, I go unto the Father.* - **John 14:28**

3. *For my Father is greater than I.* - **John 14:28**

4. *And now I have told you before it come to pass, that, when it is come to pass, ye might believe.* - **John 14:29**

5. *Hereafter I will not talk much with you.* - **John 14:30**

6. *For the prince of this world cometh.* - **John 14:30**

7. *And hath nothing in me.* - **John 14:30**

8. *But that the world may know that I love the Father.* - **John 14:31**

9. *And as the Father gave me commandment, even so I do.* - **John 14:31**

10. *Arise, let us go hence.* - **John 14:31**

November 13

JESUS SAID:

1. I am the true vine, and my Father is the husbandman. – **John 15:1**

2. Every branch in me that beareth not fruit he taketh away. – **John 15:2**

3. And every branch that beareth fruit, he purgeth it, that it may bring forth more fruit. –**John 15:2**

4. Now ye are clean through the word which I have spoken unto you. – **John 15:3**

5. Abide in me, and I in you. – **John 15:4**

6. As a branch cannot bear fruit of itself, except it abide in the vine; no more can ye, except ye abide in me. – **John 15:4**

7. I am the vine. – **John 15:5**

8. Ye are the branches. – **John 15:5**

9. He that abideth in me, and I in him, the same bringeth forth much fruit. – **John 15:5**

10. For without me, ye can do nothing. – **John 15:5**

November 14

JESUS SAID:

1. If a man abide not in me, he is cast forth as a branch.
   - **John 15:6**

2. And is withered. - **John 15:6**

3. And men gather them and cast them into the fire.
   - **John 15:6**

4. And they are burned. - **John 15:6**

5. If ye abide in me and my words abide in you, ye shall ask what ye will. - **John 15:7**

6. And it shall be done unto you. - **John 15:7**

7. Herein is my Father glorified, that ye bear much fruit.
   - **John 15:8**

8. So shall ye be my disciple. - **John 15:8**

9. As the Father hath loved me, so have I loved you. - **John 15:9**

10. Continue ye in my love. - **John 15:9**

November 15

JESUS SAID:

1. *If ye keep my commandments, ye shall abide in my love.*
   – **John 15:10**

2. *Even as I have kept my Father's commandments, and abide in his love.* – **John 15:10**

3. *These things have I spoken unto you that my joy might remain in you.* – **John 15:11**

4. *And that your joy might be full.* – **John 15:11**

5. *This is my commandment, that ye love one another, as I have loved you.* – **John 15:12**

6. *Greater love hath no man than this, that a man lay down his life for his friends.* – **John 15:13**

7. *Ye are my friends if ye do whatsoever I command you.*
   – **John 15:14**

8. *Henceforth I call you not servants.* – **John 15:15**

9. *For a servant knoweth not what his lord doeth.* – **John 15:15**

10. *But I have called you friends, for all things I have heard of my Father, I have made known unto you.* – **John 15:15**

November 16

JESUS SAID:

1. Ye have not chosen me, but I have chosen you. - **John 15:16**

2. And ordained you, that ye should go and bring forth fruit. - **John 15:16**

3. And that your fruit should remain. - **John 15:16**

4. That whatsoever ye shall ask of the Father in my name, he may give it you. - **John 15:16**

5. These things I command you, that ye love one another. - **John 15:17**

6. If the world hate you, ye know that it hated me before it hated you. - **John 15:18**

7. If ye were of the world, the world would love his own. - **John 15:19**

8. But because ye are not of the world, but I have chosen you out of the world, therefore the world hateth you. - **John 15:19**

9. Remember the word that I said unto you, the servant is not greater than his lord. - **John 15:20**

10. If they have persecuted me, they will also persecute you. - **John 15:20**

November 17

JESUS SAID:

1. If they have kept my saying, they will keep yours also. – **John 15:2**

2. But all these things will they do unto you for my name's sake. – **John 15:21**

3. Because they know not him that sent me. – **John 15:21**

4. If I had not come and spoken unto them, they had not had sin. – **John 15:22**

5. But now they have no cloak for their sin. – **John 15:22**

6. He that hateth me, hateth my Father also. – **John 15:23**

7. If I had not done among them the works which none other man did, they had not had sin. – **John 15:24**

8. But now have they both seen and hated both me and my Father. – **John 15:24**

9. But this cometh to pass, that the word might be fulfilled that is written in their law. – **John 15:25**

10. They hated me without a cause. – **John 15:25**

November 18

JESUS SAID:

1. But when the Comforter is come, whom I will send unto you from the Father. - **John 15:26**

2. Even the Spirit of truth, which proceedeth from the Father. - **John 15:26**

3. He shall testify of me. - **John 15:26**

4. And ye also shall bear witness. - **John 15:27**

5. Because ye have been with me from the beginning. - **John 15:27**;

6. These things I have spoken unto you. - **John 16:1**

7. That ye should not be offended. - **John 16:1**

8. They shall put you out of the synagogues. - **John 16:2**

9. Yea, the time cometh, that whosoever killeth you will think that he doeth God service. - **John 16:2**

10. And these things will they do unto you, because they have not known the Father, nor me. - **John 16:3**

November 19

JESUS SAID:

1. *But these things have I told you, that when the time shall come, ye may remember that I told you them.* - **John 16:4**

2. *And these things I said not unto you at the beginning, because I was with you.* - **John 16:4**

3. *But now I go my way to him that sent me.* - **John 16:5**

4. *And none of you asketh me, whither goest thou?* - **John 16:5**

5. *But because I have said these things unto you, sorrow has filled your heart.* - **John 16:6**

6. *Nevertheless, I tell you the truth.* - **John 16:7**

7. *It is expedient for you that I go away.* - **John 16:7**

8. *For if I go not away, the Comforter will not come unto you.* - **John 16:7**

9. *But if I depart, I will send him unto you.* - **John 16:7**

10. *And when he is come he will reprove the world of sin, and of righteousness and of judgment.* - **John 16:8**

November 20

JESUS SAID:

1. *Of sin, because they believe not on me; Of righteousness, because I go to my Father, and ye see me no more.*
   –John 16:9-10

2. *Of judgement, because the prince of this world is judged.*
   – John 16:11

3. *I have yet many things to say unto you.* **– John 6:12**

4. *But ye cannot hear them now.* **– John 16:12**

5. *Howbeit when he, the Spirit of truth, is come, he will guide you into all truth.* **– John 16:13**

6. *For he shall not speak of himself.* **– John 16:13**

7. *But whatsoever he shall hear, that shall he speak.* **– John 16:13**

8. *And he will shew you things to come.* **– John 16:13**

9. *He shall glorify me; for he shall receive of mine and shall shew it unto you.* **– John 16:14**

10. *All things that the Father hath are mine: therefore said, I that he shall take of mine and shall shew it unto you.* **– John 16:15**

November 21

JESUS SAID:

1. A little while and ye shall not see me. - **John 16:16**

2. And again, a little while, and ye shall see me, because I go to the Father. - **John 16:16**

3. Do ye inquire among yourselves of that I said, a little while, and ye shall not see me and again, a little while and ye shall see me? - **John 16:19**

4. Verily, verily, I say unto you, that ye shall weep and lament, but the world shall rejoice. - **John 16:20**

5. And ye shall be sorrowful, but your sorrow shall be turned into joy. - **John 16:20**

6. A woman when she is in travail hath sorrow. - **John 16:21**

7. Because her hour is come. - **John 16:21**

8. But as soon as she is delivered of the child. - **John 16:21**

9. She remembereth no more the anguish. - **John 16:21**

10. For the joy that a man is born into the world. - **John 16:21**

November 22

JESUS SAID:

1. And ye now therefore have sorrow: but I will see you again, and your heart will rejoice, and your joy no man taketh from you. In that day ye shall ask me nothing. - **John 16:22**-23

2. Verily, verily, I say unto you, whatsoever ye shall ask the Father in my name, he will give it you. - **John 16:23**

3. Hitherto have ye asked nothing in my name. - **John 16:24**

4. Ask, and ye shall receive, that your joy may be full. - **John 16:24**

5. These things have I spoken unto you in proverbs. - **John 16:25**

6. But the time cometh, when I shall no more speak unto you in proverbs. - **John 16:25**

7. But I shall shew you plainly of the Father. - **John 16:25**

8. At that day ye shall ask in my name, and I say not unto you that I will pray the Father for you. - **John 16:26**

9. For the Father himself loveth you. - **John 16:27**

10. Because ye have loved me, and believed that I came out from God. - **John 16:27**

November 23

JESUS SAID:

1. *I came forth from the Father.* - **John 16:28**

2. *And am come into the world.* - **John 16:28**

3. *Again, I leave the world.* - **John 16:28**

4. *And go to the Father.* - **John 16:28**

5. *Do ye now believe.* - **John 16:31**

6. *Behold, the hour cometh, yea, is now come.* - **John 16:32**

7. *That ye shall be scattered, every man to his own.* - **John 16:32**

8. *And shall leave me alone.* - **John 16:32**

9. *And yet I am not alone.* - **John 16:32**

10. *Because the Father is with me.* - **John 16:32**

November 24

JESUS SAID:

1. These things I have spoken unto you, that in me ye might have peace. - **John 16:33**

2. In the world ye shall have tribulations. - **John 16:33**

3. But be of good cheer. - **John 16:33**

4. I have overcome the world. - **John 16:33**

5. Father, the hour is come. - **John 17:1**

6. Glorify thy Son, that thy Son also may glorify thee. - **John 17:1**

7. As thou hast given him power over all flesh. - **John 17:2**

8. That he should give eternal life to as many as thou hast given him. - **John 17:2**

9. And this is life eternal that they might know thee. - **John 17:3**

10. The only true God, and Jesus Christ, whom thou hast sent. - **John 17:3**

November 25

JESUS SAID:

1. I have glorified thee on the earth. – **John 17:4**

2. I have finished the work which thou gavest me to do. – **John 17:4**

3. And now, O' Father, glorify thou me with thine own self with the glory which I had with thee before the world was. – **John 17:5**

4. I have manifested thy name unto the men which thou gavest me out of the world. – **John 17:6**

5. Thine they were. – **John 17:6**

6. And thou gavest them me. – **John 17:6**

7. They have kept thy word. – **John 17:6**

8. Now they have known that all things whatsoever thou hast given me are of thee. – **John 17:7**

9. For I have given unto them the words which thou gavest me. – **John 17:8**

10. And they have received them, and have known surely that I came out from thee. – **John 17:8**

November 26

JESUS SAID:

1. And they have believed that thou didst send me. - **John 17:8**

2. I pray for them. - **John 17:9**

3. I pray not for the world, but for them which thou hast given me. - **John 17:9**

4. For they are thine. - **John 17:9**

5. And all mine are thine, and thine are mine; - **John 17:10**

6. And I am glorified in them. - **John 17:10**

7. And now I am no more in the world, but these are in the world. - **John 17:11**

8. And I come to thee. - **John 17:11**

9. Holy Father, keep through thine own name those whom thou hast given me. - **John 17:11**

10. That they may be one as we are. - **John 17:11**

November 27

JESUS SAID:

1. While I was with them in the world, I kept them in thy name. – **John 17:12**

2. Those that thou gavest me I have kept. – **John 17:12**

3. And none of them is lost, but the son of perdition. – **John 17:12**

4. That the scripture might be fulfilled. – **John 17:12**

5. And now come I to thee. – **John 17:13**

6. And these things I speak in the world. – **John 17:13**

7. That they might have my joy fulfilled in themselves. – **John 17:13**

8. I have given them thy word. – **John 17:14**

9. And the world hated them. – **John 17:14**

10. Because they are not of the world, even as I am not of the world. – **John 17:14**

November 28

JESUS SAID:

1. I pray not that thou shouldest take them out of the world.
   - **John 17:15**

2. But that thou shouldest keep them from the evil. - **John 17:15**

3. They are not of the world. - **John 17:16**

4. Even as I am not of the world. - **John 17:16**

5. Sanctify them through thy truth. - **John 17:17**

6. Thy word is truth. - **John 17:17**

7. As thou hast sent me into the world. - **John 17:18**

8. Even so have I sent them into the world. - **John 17:18**

9. And for their sakes I sanctify myself. - **John 17:19**

10. That they also might be sanctified through the truth.
    - **John 17:19**

November 29

JESUS SAID:

1. Neither pray I for these alone. - **John 17:20**
2. But for them also which shall believe on me through their word. - **John 17:20**
3. That they all may be one, as thou Father, art in me, and I in thee. - **John 17:21**
4. That they also may be one in us. - **John 17:21**
5. That the world may believe that thou hast sent me. - **John 17:21**
6. And the glory which thou gavest me, I have given them. - **John 17:22**
7. That they may be one, even as we are one. - **John 17:22**
8. I in them, and thou in me. - **John 17:23**
9. That they may be made perfect in one. - **John 17:23**
10. And that the world may know that thou hast sent me, and hast loved them, as thou hast loved me. - **John 17:23**

November 30

JESUS SAID:

1. Father, I will that they also, whom thou hast given me, be with me where I am. - **John 17:24**

2. That they may behold my glory. - **John 17:24**

3. Which thou hast given me. - **John 17:24**

4. For thou lovedst me before the foundation of the world. - **John 17:24**

5. O righteous Father, the world hath not known thee. - **John 17:25**

6. But I have known thee. - **John 17:25**

7. And these have known that thou hast sent me. - **John 17:25**

8. And I have declared unto them thy name. - **John 17:26**

9. And will declare it. - **John 17:26**

10. That the love wherewith thou hast loved me may be in them and I in them. - **John 17:26**

December 1

JESUS SAID:

1. Whom seek ye? - **John 18:4**

2. I am he. - **John 18:5-6**

3. Whom seek ye? - **John 18:7**

4. I have told you that I am He. - **John 18:8**

5. If therefore ye seek Me, let these go their way. - **John 18:8**

6. Of them which thou gavest Me I have lost none. - **John 18:9**

7. Put up thy sword into the sheath. - **John 18:11**

8. The cup which my Father hath given me, shall I not drink it? - **John 18:11**

9. I spake openly to the world. - **John 18:20**

10. I even taught in the synagogue, and in the temple, whither the Jews always resort, and in secret have I said nothing. - **John 18:20**

December 2

JESUS SAID:

1. Why asked thou me? - **John 18:21**

2. Ask them which heard me, what I have said unto them. - **John 18:21**

3. Behold, they know what I said. - **John 18:21**

4. If I have spoken evil, bear witness of the evil. - **John 18:23**

5. But if well, why smitest thou me? - **John 18:23**

6. Sayest thou this thing of thyself, or did others tell it thee of me? - **John 18:34**

7. My kingdom is not of this world. - **John 18:36**

8. If my kingdom were of this world, then would my servants fight. - **John 18:36**

9. That I should not be delivered to the Jews. - **John 18:36**

10. But now is my kingdom not from hence. - **John 18:36**

December 3

JESUS SAID:

1. *Thou sayest that I am a king.* - **John 18:37**

2. *To this end was I born.* - **John 18:37**

3. *And for this cause came I into the world, that I should bear witness unto the truth.* - **John 18:37**

4. *Everyone that is of truth heareth my voice.* - **John 18:37**

5. *Thou couldest have no power at all against me except it was given thee from above.* - **John 19:11**

6. *Therefore he that delivered me unto thee hath the greater sin.* - **John 19:11**

7. *Woman, behold thy son.* - **John 19:26**

8. *Behold thy mother!* - **John 19:27**

9. *I thirst.* - **John 19:28**

10. *It is finished.* - **John 19:30**

December 4

JESUS SAID:

1. Woman, why weepest thou? - **John 20:15**

2. Whom seekest thou ? - **John 20:15**

3. Mary, touch me not. - **John 20:16**-17

4. For I am not yet ascended to my Father. - **John 20:17**

5. But go to my brethren, and say to them. - **John 20:17**

6. I ascend unto my Father, and your Father, and to God, and your God. - **John 20:17**

7. Peace be unto you. - **John 20:19**

8. Peace be unto you. - **John 20:21**

9. As my Father hath sent me. - **John 20:21**

10. Even so send I you. - **John 20:21**

December 5

JESUS SAID:

1. Receive ye the Holy Ghost. - **John 20:22**

2. Whosoever sins ye remit, they are remitted unto them. - **John 20:23**

3. And whosoever sins ye retain, they are retained. - **John 20:23**

4. Peace be unto you. - **John 20:26**

5. Reach hither thy finger, and behold my hands. - **John 20:27**

6. And reach hither thy hand, and thrust it into my side. - **John 20:27**

7. And be not faithless but believing. - **John 20:27**

8. Thomas, because thou hast seen me, thou hast believed. - **John 20:29**

9. Blessed are they that have not seen. - **John 20:29**

10. And yet have believed. - **John 20:29**

December 6

JESUS SAID:

1. Children, have ye any meat? - **John 21:5**

2. Cast the net on the right side of the ship, and ye shall find. - **John 21:6**

3. Bring of the fish which ye have now caught. - **John 21:10**

4. Come and dine. - **John 21:12**

5. Simon, son of Jonas, lovest thou me more than these? - **John 21:15**

6. Feed my lambs. - **John 21:15**

7. Simon, son of Jonas, lovest thou me? - **John 21:16**

8. Feed my sheep. - **John 21:16**

9. Simon son of Jonas, lovest thou me? - **John 21:17**

10. Feed my sheep. - **John 21:17**

December 7

JESUS SAID:

1. Verily, verily, I say unto thee. – **John 21:18**

2. When thou wast young, thou girdedst thyself, and walkedst whither thou wouldest. – **John 21:18**

3. But when thou shalt be old, thou shalt stretch forth thy hands, and another shall gird thee, and carry thee whither thou wouldest not. Follow me. – **John 21:18**-19

4. If I will that he tarry till I come. – **John 21:22**,23

5. What that to thee? – **John 21:22**

6. Follow thou me. – **John 21:22**

7. (Wait for the promise of the Father), Which, ye have heard of me. – **Acts 1:4**

8. For John truly baptized with water, but ye shall be baptized with the Holy Ghost not many days hence. It is not for you to know the times or the seasons, which the Father hath put in his own power. – **Acts 1:5,7**

9. But ye shall receive power after that the Holy Ghost is come upon you. – **Acts 1:8**

10. And ye shall be witnesses unto me both in Jerusalem and in all Judea and in Samaria and unto the uttermost part of the earth. – **Acts 1:8**

December 8

JESUS SAID:

1. Saul, Saul, why persecutest thou me? - **Acts 9:4**

2. I am Jesus whom thou persecutest. - **Acts 9:5**

3. It is hard for thee to kick against the pricks. - **Acts 9:5**

4. Arise and go into the city, and it shall be told thee what thou must do. - **Acts 9:6**

5. Ananias, arise and go into the street which is called Straight. - **Acts 9:10-11**

6. And inquire in the house of Judas for one called Saul, of Tarsus; for, behold, he prayeth. - **Acts 9:11**

7. And has seen in a vision a man named Ananias coming in, and putting his hand on him that he might receive his sight. - **Acts 9:12**

8. Go thy way: for he is a chosen vessel unto me, to bear my name before the Gentiles, and kings, and the children of Israel. - **Acts 9:15**

9. For I will shew him how great things he must suffer. - **Acts 9:16**

10. For my name's sake. - **Acts 9:16**

December 9

JESUS SAID:

1. Rise, Peter, kill and eat. - **Acts 10:13**

2. What God hath cleansed, that call not thou common. - **Acts 10:15**

3. Arise, Peter, slay and eat. - **Acts 11:7**

4. What God hath cleansed, that call not thou common. - **Acts 11:9**

5. John indeed baptized with water. - **Acts 11:16**

6. But ye shall be baptized with the Holy Ghost. - **Acts 11:16**

7. Be not afraid, but speak, and hold not thy peace. - **Acts 18:9**

8. For I am with thee. - **Acts 18:10**

9. And no man shall set on thee to hurt thee. - **Acts 18:10**

10. For I have much people in this city. - **Acts 18:10**

December 10

JESUS SAID:

1. It is more blessed to give than to receive. - **Acts 20:35**

2. Saul, Saul, why persecutest thou me? - **Acts 22:7**

3. I am Jesus of Nazareth, whom thou persecutest. - **Acts 22:8**

4. Arise and go into Damascus. - **Acts 22:10**

5. And there it shall be told thee of all things which are appointed for thee to do. - **Acts 22:10**

6. Make haste, and get thee quickly out of Jerusalem. - **Acts 22:18**

7. For they will not receive thy testimony concerning me. - **Acts 22:18**

8. Depart, for I will send thee far hence unto the Gentiles. - **Acts 22:21**

9. Be of good cheer, Paul, for as thou hast testified of me in Jerusalem. - **Acts 23:11**

10. So must thou bear witness also at Rome. - **Acts 23:11**

December 11
JESUS SAID:

1. Saul, Saul, why persecutest thou me? - **Acts 26:14**

2. It is hard for thee to kick against the pricks. - **Acts 26:14**

3. I am Jesus whom thou persecutest. - **Acts 26:15**

4. But rise and stand upon thy feet. - **Acts 26:16**

5. For I have appeared unto thee for this purpose. - **Acts 26:16**

6. To make thee a minister and a witness both of these things which thou hast seen. - **Acts 26:16**

7. And of those things in which I will appear unto thee. - **Acts 26:16**

8. Delivering thee from the people, and from the Gentiles, unto whom now I send thee. - **Acts 26:17**

9. To open their eyes, and to turn them from darkness to light, and from the power of Satan unto God. - **Acts 26:18**

10. That they may receive forgiveness of sins and inheritance among them which are sanctified by faith that is in me. - **Acts 26:18**

December 12

JESUS SAID:

1. Take, eat: this is my body, which is broken for you.
   - **I Corinthians 11:24**

2. This do in remembrance of me. - **I Corinthians 11:24**

3. This cup is the new testament in my blood.
   - **I Corinthians 11:25**

4. This do ye, as oft as ye drink it, in remembrance of me.
   - **I Corinthians 11:25**

5. My grace is sufficient for thee. - **II Corinthians 12:9**

6. For my strength is made perfect in weakness.
   - **II Corinthians 12:9**

7. The labourer is worthy of his hire. - **Luke 10:7**

8. I am Alpha and Omega. - **Revelation 1:8**

9. The beginning and the ending. - **Revelation 1:8**

10. I am Alpha and Omega, the first and the last. - **Revelation 1:11**

December 13

JESUS SAID:

1. What thou seest write in a book. - **Revelation 1:11**

2. And send it to the seven churches which are in Asia. - **Revelation 1:11**

3. Unto Ephesus, and unto Smyrna, and unto Pergamos, and unto Thyatira, and unto Sardis and unto Philadelphia, and unto Laodicea. - **Revelation 1:11**

4. Fear not; I am the first and the last : I am he that liveth, and was dead. - **Revelation 1:17-18**

5. And behold, I am alive for evermore, - **Revelation 1:18**

6. Amen. - **Revelation 1:18**

7. And have the keys of hell and of death. - **Revelation 1:18**

8. Write the things which thou hast seen. - **Revelation 1:19**

9. And the things which are. - **Revelation 1:19**

10. And the things which shall be hereafter. - **Revelation 1:19**

December 14

JESUS SAID:

1. *The mystery of the seven stars which thou sawest in my right hand, and the seven golden candlesticks.* - **Revelation 1:20**

2. *The seven stars are angels of the seven churches.* - **Revelation 1:20**

3. *And the seven candlesticks which thou sawest are the seven churches.* - **Revelation 1:20**

4. *Unto the angel of the church of Ephesus write.* - **Revelation 2:1**

5. *These things saith he that holdeth the seven stars in his right hand.* - **Revelation 2:1**

6. *Who walketh in the midst of the seven golden candlesticks.* - **Revelation 2:1**

7. *I know thy works and thy labour, and thy patience.* - **Revelation 2:2**

8. *And how thou canst not bear them which are evil:* - **Revelation 2:2**

9. *And thou hast tried them which say they are apostles, and are not.* - **Revelation 2:2**

10. *And has found them liars:* - **Revelation 2:2**

December 15

JESUS SAID:

1. And hast borne, and hast patience. - **Revelation 2:3**

2. And for my name's sake hast laboured, - **Revelation 2:3**

3. And hast not fainted. - **Revelation 2:3**

4. Nevertheless, I have somewhat against thee, - **Revelation 2:4**

5. Because thou hast left thy first love. - **Revelation 2:4**

6. Remember therefore from whence thou art fallen, and repent. - **Revelation 2:5**

7. And do the first works; - **Revelation 2:5**

8. Or else I will come unto thee quickly,- **Revelation 2:5**

9. And I will remove thy candlestick out of his place, - **Revelation 2:5**

10. Except thou repent. - **Revelation 2:5**

December 16
JESUS SAID:

1. But this thou hast, that thou hatest the deeds of the Nicolaitans, which I also hate. - **Revelation 2:6**

2. He that hath an ear, let him hear what the Spirit saith unto the churches; - **Revelation 2:7**

3. To him that overcometh will I give to eat of the tree of life, - **Revelation 2:7**

4. Which is in the midst of the paradise of God. - **Revelation 2:7**

5. And unto the angel of the church in Smyrna write; - **Revelation 2:8**

6. These things saith the first and the last, - **Revelation 2:8**

7. Which was dead, and is alive; - **Revelation 2:8**

8. I know thy works, and tribulation, and poverty, - **Revelation 2:9**

10. And I know the blasphemy of them which say they are Jews, and are not, but are the synagogue of Satan. - **Revelation 2:9**

December 17

JESUS SAID:

1. *Fear none of those things which thou shalt suffer:* – **Revelation 2:10**

2. *Behold, the devil shall cast some of you into prison, that ye may be tried;* – **Revelation 2:10**

3. *And ye shall have tribulation ten days:* – **Revelation 2:10**

4. *Be thou faithful unto death,* – **Revelation 2:10**

5. *And I will give thee the crown of life.* – **Revelation 2:10**

6. *He that hath an ear, let him hear what the Spirit saith unto the churches;* – **Revelation 2:11**

7. *He that overcometh shall not be hurt of the second death.* – **Revelation 2:11**

8. *And to the angel of the church in Pergamos write;* – **Revelation 2:12**

9. *These things saith he which hath the sharp sword with two edges;* – **Revelation 2:12**

10. *I know thou works and where thou dwellest.* – **Revelation 2:13**

December 18

JESUS SAID:

1. I know thy works and where thou dwellest even where Satan's seat is: - **Revelation 2:13**

2. And thou holdest fast my name, - **Revelation 2:13**

3. And hast not denied my faith, - **Revelation 2:13**

4. Even in those days wherein Antipas was my faithful martyr, who was slain among you, where Satan dwelleth. - **Revelation 2:13**

5. But I have a few things against thee, - **Revelation 2:14**

6. Because thou hast there them that hold the doctrine of Balaam, who taught Balac to cast a stumbling block before the children of Israel, - **Revelation 2:14**

7. To eat things sacrificed unto idols, - **Revelation 2:14**

8. And to commit fornication. - **Revelation 2:14**

9. So hast thou also them that hold the doctrine of the Nicolaitans, - **Revelation 2:15**

10. Which thing I hate. - **Revelation 2:15**

December 19

JESUS SAID:

1. Repent; or else I will come unto thee quickly, - **Revelation 2:16**
2. And will fight against them with the sword of my mouth. - **Revelation 2:16**
3. He that hath an ear, let him hear what the Spirit saith unto the churches; - **Revelation 2:17**
4. To him that overcometh will I give to eat of the hidden manna, - **Revelation 2:17**
5. And I will give him a white stone. - **Revelation 2:17**
6. And in the stone a new name written, - **Revelation 2:17**
7. Which no man knoweth saving he that receiveth it. - **Revelation 2:17**
8. And unto the angel of the church at Thyatira write ; - **Revelation 2:18**
9. These things saith the Son of God, - **Revelation 2:18**
10. Who hath his eyes like unto a flame of fire, and his feet are like fine brass ; - **Revelation 2:18**

December 20

JESUS SAID:

1. I know thy works and charity, and service, and faith,
   - **Revelation 2:19**

2. And thy patience, and thy works ; - **Revelation 2:19**

3. And the last to be more than the first. - **Revelation 2:19**

4. Notwithstanding I have a few things against thee,
   - **Revelation 2:20**

5. Because thou sufferest that woman Jezebel, which calleth herself a prophetess, to teach and seduce my servants to commit fornication, and to eat things sacrificed unto idols.
   - **Revelation 2:20**

6. And I gave her space to repent of her fornication; and she repented not. - **Revelation 2:21**

7. Behold, I will cast her into a bed,- **Revelation 2:22**

8. And them that commit adultery with her into great tribulation, except they repent of their deeds.
   - **Revelation 2:22**

9. And I will kill her children with death; - **Revelation 2:23**

10. And all the churches shall know that I am he which searches the reins and hearts: and I will give unto every one of you according to your works. - **Revelation 2:23**

December 21

JESUS SAID:

1. But unto you, I say, and unto the rest in Thyatira, as many as have not this doctrine, - **Revelation 2:24**

2. And which have not known the depths of Satan, as they speak; - **Revelation 2:24**

3. I will put upon you none other burden. - **Revelation 2:24**

4. But that which ye have already hold fast till I come. - **Revelation 2:25**

5. And he that overcometh, and keepeth my works unto the end, - **Revelation 2:26**

6. To him will I give power over the nations: - **Revelation 2:26**

7. And he shall rule them with a rod of iron; - **Revelation 2:27**

8. As the vessels of a potter shall they be broken to shivers: - **Revelation 2:27**

9. Even as I received of my Father. - **Revelation 2:27**

10. And I will give him the morning star. - **Revelation 2:28**

December 22

JESUS SAID:

1. He that hath an ear, let him hear what the Spirit saith unto the churches. - **Revelation 2:29**
2. And unto the angel of the church in Sardis write ; - **Revelation 3:1**
3. These things saith he hath the seven Spirits of God, and the seven stars; I know thy works. - **Revelation 3:1**
4. That thou hast a name that thou livest, and art dead. - **Revelation 3:1**
5. Be watchful, and strengthen the things which remain, that are ready to die: - **Revelation 3:2**
6. For I have not found thy works perfect before God. - **Revelation 3:2**
7. Remember therefore how thou hast received and heard, and hold fast, and repent. - **Revelation 3:3**
8. If therefore thou shalt not watch, I will come on thee as a thief, - **Revelation 3:3**
9. And thou shalt not know what hour I will come upon thee. - **Revelation 3:3**
10. Thou hast a few names even in Sardis which have not defiled their garments ; and they shall walk with me in white : for they are worthy. - **Revelation 3:4**

December 23
JESUS SAID:

1. He that overcometh, the same shall be clothed in white raiment ; - **Revelation 3:5**

2. And I will not blot out his name out of the book of life, - **Revelation 3:5**

3. But I will confess his name before my Father, and before his angels. - **Revelation 3:5**

4. He that hath an ear, let him hear what the Spirit saith unto the churches. - **Revelation 3:6**

5. And to the angel of the church in Philadelphia write; - **Revelation 3:7**

6. These things saith he that is holy, - **Revelation 3:7**

7. He that is true, - **Revelation 3:7**

8. He that hath the key of David, - **Revelation 3:7**

9. He that openeth, and no man shutteth; and shutteth, and no man openeth ; - **Revelation 3:7**

10. I know thy works: - **Revelation 3:8**

December 24

JESUS SAID:

1. Behold, I have set before thee an open door, - **Revelation 3:8**

2. And no man can shut it: - **Revelation 3:8**

3. For thou hast a little strength, - **Revelation 3:8**

4. And hast kept my word, - **Revelation 3:8**

5. And hast not denied my name. - **Revelation 3:8**

6. Behold, I will make of them of the synagogue of Satan, - **Revelation 3:9**

7. Which say they are Jews, and are not, but do lie; - **Revelation 3:9**

8. Behold, I will make them to come and worship before thy feet, - **Revelation 3:9**

9. And to know that I have loved thee. - **Revelation 3:9**

10. Because thou hast kept the word of my patience, - **Revelation 3:10**

December 25

JESUS SAID:

1. I also will keep thee from the hour of temptation, which shall come upon all of the world, - **Revelation 3:10**

2. To try them that dwell upon the earth. - **Revelation 3:10**

3. Behold, I come quickly: - **Revelation 3:11**

4. Hold fast which thou hast, - **Revelation 3:11**

5. That no man take thy crown. - **Revelation 3:11**

6. Him that overcometh will I make a pillar in the temple of my God, - **Revelation 3:12**

7. And he shall go no more out: - **Revelation 3:12**

8. And I will write upon him the name of my God, - **Revelation 3:12**

9. And the name of the city of my God, - **Revelation 3:12**

10. Which is new Jerusalem, which cometh down out of Heaven from my God: and I will write upon him my new name. - **Revelation 3:12**

December 26

JESUS SAID:

1. He that hath an ear, let him hear what the Spirit saith unto the churches. - **Revelation 3:13**

2. And unto the angel of the church of the Laodiceans write; - **Revelation 3:14**

3. These things saith the Amen, - **Revelation 3:14**

4. The faithful and true witnesses, - **Revelation 3:14**

5. The beginning of the creation of God; - **Revelation 3:14**

6. I know thy works, - **Revelation 3:15**

7. That thou art neither cold or hot : - **Revelation 3:15**

8. I would thou wert cold or hot. - **Revelation 3:15**

9. So then because thou art lukewarm, and neither cold nor hot, - **Revelation 3:16**

10. I will spew thee out of my mouth. - **Revelation 3:16**

December 27

JESUS SAID:

1. Because thou sayest, I am rich, and increased with goods and have need of nothing; – **Revelation 3:17**

2. And knowest not that thou are wretched, and miserable, and poor, and blind, and naked : – **Revelation 3:17**

3. I counsel thee to buy of me gold tried in the fire, – **Revelation 3:18**

4. That thou mayest be rich; – **Revelation 3:18**

5. And white raiment, that thou mayest be clothed, – **Revelation 3:18**

6. And that the shame of thy nakedness do not appear;. – **Revelation 3:18**

7. And anoint thine eyes with eye-salve, that thou mayest see. – **Revelation 3:18**

8. As many as I love, I rebuke and chasten: – **Revelation 3:19**

9. Be zealous therefore, and repent. – **Revelation 3:19**

10. Behold, I stand at the door, and knock : if any man hear my voice, and open the door, I will come in to him, and will sup with him, and he with me. – **Revelation 3:20**

December 28

JESUS SAID:

1. To him that overcometh will I grant to sit with me in my throne, - **Revelation 3:21**

2. Even as I also overcame, - **Revelation 3:21**

3. And am set down with my Father in his throne. - **Revelation 3:21**

4. He that hath an ear, let him hear what the Spirit saith unto the churches. - **Revelation 3:22**

5. Behold, I come as a thief. - **Revelation 16:15**

6. Blessed is he that watcheth, - **Revelation 16:15**

7. And keepeth his garments, lest he walk naked, - **Revelation 16:15**

8. And they see his shame. - **Revelation 16:15**

9. Behold, I come quickly : - **Revelation 22:7**

10. Blessed is he that keepeth the sayings of the prophecy of this book. - **Revelation 22:7**

December 29

JESUS SAID:

1. And behold I come quickly; - **Revelation 22:12**

2. And my reward is with me, - **Revelation 22:12**

3. To give every man according as his work shall be. - **Revelation 22:12**

4. I am Alpha and Omega. - **Revelation 22:13**

5. The beginning and the end, - **Revelation 22:13**

6. The first and the last. - **Revelation 22:13**

7. I Jesus have sent mine angel to testify unto you these things in the churches. - **Revelation 22:16**

8. I am the root and the offspring of David. - **Revelation 22:16**

9. And the bright and morning star. - **Revelation 22:16**

10. Surely I come quickly. - **Revelation 22:20**

December 30
JESUS SAID:

1. The laborer is worthy of his reward. - **1 Timothy 5:18**

2. My grace is sufficient for thee. - **II Corinthians 12:9**

3. For my strength is made perfect in weakness. - **II Corinthians 12:9**

4. Be not afraid, but speak, and hold not thy peace. - **Acts 18:9**

5. For I am with thee. - **Acts 18:10**

6. And no man shall set on thee to hurt thee. - **Acts 18:10**

7. For I have much people in this city. - **Acts 18:10**

8. Which ye have heard of me. - **Acts 1:4**

9. For John truly baptized with water. - **Acts 1:5**

10. But ye shall be baptized with the Holy Ghost not many days hence. - **Acts 1:5**

December 31

JESUS SAID:

1. *It is not for you to know the time or seasons.* - **Acts 1:7**

2. *Which the Father hath put in his own power.* - **Acts 1:7**

3. *But ye shall receive power, after that the Holy Ghost is come upon you.* - **Acts 1:8**

4. *And ye shall be witnesses unto me both in Jerusalem, and in all Judaea, and in Samaria.* - **Acts 1:8**

5. *And unto the uttermost part of the earth.* - **Acts 1:8**

6. *If I will that he tarry till I come, what is that to thee?* - **John 21: 22, 23**

7. *I have sent mine angel to testify unto you these things in the churches.* - **Revelation 22:16**

8. *I am the root and offspring of David.* - **Revelation 22:16**

9. *And the bright and morning star.* - **Revelation 22:16**

10. *Surely, I come quickly.* - **Revelation 22:20**

Made in United States
Orlando, FL
20 November 2024